Late Bloomer

TidePool Press
Cambridge, Massachusetts

For Jewelle

Acknowledgments

A SMALL BUT mighty group of people encouraged me in the writing of this memoir. It simply would not have happened without the constant, unflagging encouragement of my wonderful wife, Jewelle, over the last almost twenty years it has taken me to write it. Her enthusiasm never faltered and her suggestions were always insightful. The book also would not have happened without the relentless encouragement of my friend and agent, Phyllis Wender; it was her idea that there was a book in my story.

But, there were many others. I took June Foley's superb class in memoir writing at the New School and several of my classmates and I continued to meet and discuss our work long after the class had ended, discussions that are reflected in the book. They include: Brian Morgan, Debby Haney, Jana Sladkova, Elizabeth Ann Sawyer and Kim Chase. There were friends who were kind enough to read and comment on early drafts: Llewelyn Jones

Nicholas, who is featured in the book and didn't complain about how I treated her; Susan Jonas, Patricia Levinson and Brook Berlind, whose insights and comments on aspects of the drafts they read led me to make important changes; Aaron Latham, excellent novelist himself who was the first person to alert me to the fact that some of my earlier memories that crowded the first eighty pages of the draft he read were not interesting to people who aren't related to me, and maybe even if they are.

My friend Gabriella De Ferrari, the author of one of the best memoirs I've ever read, *Gringa Latina*, helped me over the hurdle of understanding how a memoirist can create dialogue but retain emotional truth, an understanding that was greatly furthered by William Zinsser's essential book, *Inventing the Truth*. Gabriella's son and my friend Nathaniel Jeppson is solely responsible for finding me Jock Herron and TidePool Press without which you would not have this splendid volume in your hands. My deepest thanks to Jock; his brother, Frank Herron, whose eagle eye removed many imperfections from the text and whose painstaking research improved its accuracy enormously; and to Ingrid Mach, who designed this book with great creativity and sensitivity.

My daughter Laura Bickford persuaded me to turn the story into a film script in order to impose discipline on my unruly and uneven manuscript. I followed her advice and, with her creative help, shortened, organized and shaped the narrative. My daughter Emily Lansbury read the early drafts with a wonderful sensitivity that helped me think about my boyhood in what I hope is a clear and unsentimental way. My friend Lesley Stahl led me to Bill Phillips, editor *extraordinaire*, who guided me in many important ways including steering me away from writing a novel based on my experiences toward the tougher but, I came to understand, better memoir form. Although Bill helped me enormously, he isn't responsible for the result, nor are any of the other wonderful friends and members of my family who have so indulgently helped me over the years and to whom I am very grateful. Only I am responsible for any errors or omissions, of which I am sure there are many.

"Family life itself, that safest, most traditional, most approved of female choices, is not a sanctuary: It is, perpetually, a dangerous place."

Margaret Drabble, in her review of Mary Gordon's *Men and Angels*, in *The New York Times*, Sunday, March 31, 1985

"I'm not going to tell the story the way it happened. I'm going to tell it the way I remember it."

Mitch Glazer, in his script for the 20th Century Fox film of Dickens' *Great Expectations*, 1998

Late Bloomer

Chapter One

THE FIRST TIME I saw Phillips Exeter Academy was at my older brother Bob's graduation in June 1952. The drive with Mom and Dad up to New Hampshire from our house in Ardsley-on-Hudson, about twenty miles north of New York City, is a little hazy now that I'm past the middle of my seventh decade on Earth. I do remember that it was sunny and hot. When we got there, Dad parked our green Ford station wagon with wooden side panels, got out and told me to get moving. There was a parade about to start somewhere, he said, and he wanted to be in it. He took off his seersucker jacket, which was wrinkled and wet with sweat, rolled up the sleeves of his white button-down shirt and loosened his red and white striped Exeter tie. He fumbled around in the back of the car for a moment and retrieved a straw hat—a "boater"he called it—with a red and white Class of 1920 band around the crown. He put in on at a rakish angle and grabbed me by the arm. "Let's go," he said. Mom called that she'd hold seats for us.

A group of men and boys was milling around one side of what appeared to be the main building on the campus. Dad told me it was the Academy Building. It was a red brick, ivy-covered building with white-painted windows that looked like about seven or eight other buildings I could see clustered around and in back of it, but it was longer and larger and had a white cupola. I saw women and kids standing on the lawn under the tall trees in front of the Academy Building where folding chairs had been set up on the grass facing a long wooden stage with a speaker's rostrum in the center built for the occasion. Dad dragged me toward a group that was slowly congealing into a disorganized line. We joined with about a dozen men and boys who turned out to be Dad's classmates and their kids. Then, with a larger group from many different classes, we all started off behind a huge drum on wheels that was being flogged in march time by a student dressed in white pants and shoes and a red jacket. No band; just the drum. Boom, boom.

We walked—not marched—behind the drum all through the campus passing a lot of old brick buildings, most all of them covered with ivy, joined by crisscrossing cement walks and surrounded everywhere by big, leafy trees. As we walked by one of the older buildings, Dad pointed at it and said that it was Hoyt Hall, where Bob had lived during his senior year. Dad didn't say much to me. He was busy catching up with a couple of the men he hadn't seen in years. So, I looked at all the buildings we passed and the trees and the little town with white-painted stores. I recognized some names Bob had mentioned, such as George &

Phillips where he bought shirts. We passed a hamburger joint named Bill's I thought I'd probably get to know better. It was a pretty small town. The sun was blazing. It was really hot. Dad and most of the men had taken off their jackets and were carrying them slung over their shoulders; ties were at half-mast. We circled back to the front of the Academy Building where we saw Mom standing in front of three chairs she'd been holding for us. The marchers dissolved into the seats. I fumbled in my pocket to make sure the graduation present I'd gotten for Bob was still there.

I'd bought him a Bulova wristwatch at Reich's Jewelry in Dobbs Ferry as a graduation present. It cost so much that I used a ten-dollar bill I got from an uncle at Christmas as a down payment and then promised to pay Mr. Reich most of my allowance for what seemed like the rest of my life. When he understood the state of my finances, he agreed that if I paid at least forty-five of the sixty-two dollars the watch cost with Bob's initials and the date of his graduation engraved on the back, he'd let me take it to the graduation in its purple velvet box and I could pay him the rest later. I gave him the whole amount by the end of May. When I'd told her my plan, Mom had paid me to do a lot of useless chores around the house like feeding the tropical fish and letting our two dachshunds out in the morning or something else I was already supposed to be doing but usually didn't unless she paid me.

The graduation ceremony was long and boring, especially after we saw Bob climb up on the stage and get his diploma from Principal William G. Saltonstall—"Salty" to Dad who had known him when they both were at Harvard—and then had to watch all the other seniors we didn't know do the same thing. There must have been way over a hundred of them. I noticed that the white-haired Principal did a quick double take when he shook Bob's hand as he gave him his diploma. He couldn't have known Bob all that well because he didn't seem to know that Bob had a problem with his right hand—a birth injury that left him with a slightly withered right arm and hand.

Mom made a big fuss over Bob, kissing and hugging him and telling him how grown up he looked in his black cap and gown and how proud she was. Bob looked irritated by all her gushing and seemed to want to break away; he was agitated and kept looking around for something. I thought it was funny, and was waiting for him to stop moving around so I could give him my present. Dad shook Bob's hand and, in a very serious voice, told him that he'd done a fine job at Exeter and that he was very, very proud of him. Dad took an envelope from the inside pocket of his jacket and handed it to Bob.

"Jeeeez...us!" Bob yelled, looking at the note and waving a check. "I can't believe it! Thanks Dad!"

His face was flushed and excited, and he bolted away from us with his black gown billowing around him and ran over to one group of parents and siblings surrounding one of his classmates and then to another. "I'm going!" he bellowed, jumping up and down.

"My goodness, he's excited," Mom said to Dad. "I didn't think you were going to let him go. When did you change your mind? What did you tell him?"

"I told him about two months ago that if he kept his nose to the grindstone, maybe, just maybe, I'd give him the money today and then he could go. I didn't want him to sluff off the last term thinking he was definitely going to Europe. 'Senior Slump' is bad enough."

"Two months ago? And you never said anything to me? Not a *word*?"

Dad didn't answer and turned away from her.

"What's this about Europe?" I asked him.

"I'm going to let Bob take one of those student ships to Rotterdam and travel around Europe this summer with some of his friends from school. I guess those boys"—he pointed at Bob whooping it up—"are part of the group."

"Oh," I said. "I didn't know that. How long's he going for?"

"Most of the summer. He leaves after the Fourth of July and gets back just before Harvard opens in September."

"He's not really old enough, Dear," Mom said to him in her pinched, tight way she used when she was unhappy about something. "You could have told me you were going to let him go. Why didn't you at least tell me?"

Dad didn't answer. He just turned away from her again with a sour look on his face like he'd swallowed a bug and started walking to the parking lot where he'd left the station wagon. After a few moments, Mom looked at me and shrugged as if to say well, I guess there's nothing I can do about it, and began following Dad. I stuffed the velvet box I'd been holding behind me into the pocket of my jacket and followed her.

As I neared the car, I could hear Mom's voice. "But, why? I've never been to Europe and you know how much I want to go. Why Bobby? He's so young." Dad didn't say anything. He fumbled with the keys and paid no attention to her. She tried again.

"Well I don't think it's right. Bobby's not even seventeen yet. And you know I've wanted to go all my life."

"Drop it," he whispered sharply to her.

"At least you could have told me," she said.

"Drop it, NOW," he grunted angrily.

I got in the back seat as if I didn't know anything was wrong. Then Bob came racing over to the car. Still jumping around and excited, he stuck his head inside and kissed Mom and waved and yelled thanks again to Dad. He'd begun to race off again when Mom called to him to come back.

"Your brother's got a present for you," she shouted.

Bob came back and asked me what the present was as I was trying to retrieve the package from my pocket.

"A watch."

"Hey, that's great. Thanks a lot," he said as I passed him the velvet box through the window. He didn't open it. Instead, he stuffed it in his pocket and ran off.

"Wasn't that a cute thing for your brother to do, Dear? He's been saving for months," Mom called to Bob as he was racing off, although he'd already gone. Mom turned around in the front seat and faced me, smiling, "You know, you really are a very thoughtful boy," she said, roughing up my hair. "Your buying the watch for Bob reminded me of the pin you bought me for Christmas years ago at the church fair. Do you remember that?" she asked, smiling like I was oh-so-cute.

Yes, I remembered that pin, too, but I wasn't smiling. I felt like crying, but I couldn't do that. I was twelve years old—too old to cry. I hadn't cried in years.

Chapter Two

AFTER HIS GRADUATION from Exeter, Bob was in high spirits planning his trip to Europe. Dad and Mom stayed mad at each other, in their repressed way, about the trip, meaning that they didn't talk to each other except when they had to—like "dinner is ready" or "please change the channel while you're up." Otherwise, they existed in silence and Bob and I did too, whenever we were around them.

The nights were torture. Bob and I could feel our parents' anger everywhere in the house. It was in every corner, in every breath of air. We both knew that it had to be much more than just Bob's trip that was wrong, although the trip had become a festering sore. One night at dinner, after her usual three gins with ice had transformed her into my Night Mother—an entirely different person than she was during the day—she asked Dad, "...Why, why are you letting Bobby go? He's still only a child and I've been waiting all my life to go to Europe?"

At first, he growled, "...too busy at the office and can't take the time." After Mom didn't say anything, he added, "Also, it would be much more expensive for the two of us to go than just Bob alone."

"How much money are you going to give him," she asked?

No answer.

"Why couldn't we save whatever you were going to give Bobby and the two of us can go next year," she asked?

No answer.

"Why are you doing this," she almost choked?

After a long moment, he hissed "quit harping on it" and raised his hand as if to strike out at her. Then he brought his hand slowly to the back of his head, stroked his hair a few times glowering at her with smoldering rage, got up from the table and left the room.

We didn't say anything, of course; we never did. We tried to go on as if everything was normal, breathing the poison fog. I watched television as late as possible every night to avoid going to bed knowing that I'd worry about how Mom and Dad seemed to hate each other. What if they got a divorce? Where would I live? What would Mom do for money? She didn't have a penny of her own. Dad gave her an allowance for the basics, more than mine, of course, but still she had to ask Dad for everything. She didn't even know how much she and Dad had in the bank. She told me she'd asked him many times if they had any savings or stocks, or anything, but he wouldn't tell her. She'd stopped asking a long time ago.

Bob and I became robots, going through the motions of eating and watching television at night with them, the four of us in the same room, each of us in our own worlds, not speaking or touching, not even looking at each other. Dad would go upstairs to bed first. He'd get up from his armchair and walk out of the room without saying anything, but then we'd hear his feet on the stairs. Sometimes, I'd say "good night" to him as he left. Sometimes he'd grunt; I don't remember him answering. Mom would stay for a while with her glassy eyes glued to the tube until she'd polished off her last drop of gin. Then she'd put her glass down ever so slowly and struggle out of her chair. Bent over like an old woman, she would stagger over to Bob or me and mumble something we often didn't understand but took to mean that she was going upstairs to bed. Then she'd lurch off out of the room and we'd hear her stumbling up the stairs, sometimes missing one and half-falling until she grabbed the banister and regained her balance. How I hated that nightly transformation, but had no power to stop it. I'd watch with horror as she drank one drink and, in the course of the second drink—a space of no more than ten minutes—she'd change totally. An entirely different person would put down that second drink, a person with a different identity, emotions, vocabulary and even with different looks. With that second drink, her head would roll forward and she'd hunch her shoulders. The look in her eyes was old.

DAD WAS BORN in December 1901 and lived most of the time when he was young on Staten Island. His father, who died before I was born, was a lawyer in New York City, a partner of the famous Joseph Choate—my uncle Joe was named after him. Dad didn't talk much about what it was like living on Staten Island

and said he really grew up on his father's farm in Colebrook, a very small town in northwestern Connecticut, where he spent the summers, although that was hard to imagine. I remember him always dressed in a suit and vest, looking as if he was about to argue a case before the Supreme Court. He was also completely useless around the house. He'd gone to Exeter, Class of 1920, Harvard College, Class of 1924, and Harvard Law School, Class of 1927. He went to work at Simpson Thacher & Bartlett in New York City right out of law school in 1927 and never worked anywhere else.

I found a wrinkled photograph of Dad, probably taken in the early 1930's, in a drawer in a big chest in our living room under a stack of old letters. There he was, sitting in the driver's seat of a big, old-fashioned car with the top down. He was wearing a floppy hat. One hand was on the steering wheel. His left leg was dangling over the door outside the car. There was a girl I didn't recognize in the front seat next to him and a couple I didn't know in the back seat. The girls were wearing flapper hats that looked like helmets and everybody was laughing. Dad was smirking like he was King of the Hill, a real sport. I didn't recognize the Dad in that photograph. Maybe, it had been taken during Prohibition when drinking was wicked and fun and you went to places with little slots in the doors and said a password to get in. Maybe, that's where Dad was going with those girls. I stopped thinking about it because the picture just didn't fit. There wasn't much fun left in him now, if there ever had been any.

I kept rummaging around in the drawer looking for other pictures of Dad and found, instead, some large sepia photographs of Mom on the bottom under everything else, turned face downward. They were portraits, also taken in the mid-1930's I guessed. Of course, I knew right away that it was Mom, but I couldn't account for how her looks had changed. Comparing those old photographs with my Day Mother, there was an unmistakable resemblance, although the youthfully sharp features in the pictures had softened and become puffy. Comparing those pictures with my Night Mother was altogether a different matter. The open and innocent eyes in the photographs at night became glassy and impenetrable, dead, covered by her eyelids at half-mast. The prominent cheekbones of the Mom in the pictures were now hidden under sagging, bloated flesh. How could the innocent beauty smiling at me from those sepia photographs ever have evolved into the mother I knew? I was sure that she'd hidden the photographs, buried them under piles of old letters and other things accumulated over many years, unwilling to let go of them completely, but keeping them out of sight so she would not have to face her visible disintegration, like a reverse Dorian Gray.

How I wanted to know the two strangers in those photographs.

BOB'S TRIP WAS cancelled only a few days before he was supposed to leave. The ship, an old wartime troop transport, had finally collapsed and died in port in Holland and there was no replacement. Dad never considered paying the huge extra expense for Bob to fly. His trip was off.

Bob's spirits crashed. Dreaming about the trip he'd planned so carefully had been holding him together. He'd scotch-taped a huge *National Geographic* map of Europe to his bedroom wall and had traced the main routes and side trips he wanted to take with crayons of various colors. He'd written away for train and ferry schedules and ticket prices and had stacks of timetables and tourist brochures all over his room. His big, red plaid fabric suitcase, half-packed since a week after he'd returned from Exeter, sat on the armchair in the corner of his room.

Bob pored over the telegram giving him the bad news, searching for some hope, some hidden meaning different from the clear message that his trip would not happen.

"It's a joke, dammit. Some asshole thinks this is really funny, I'll bet you anything. Because it's impossible that they could do this. It's goddamn IMPOSSIBLE," he screamed. "Did you have anything to do with this…this thing?" he asked me, holding the hated telegram with two fingers as far away from his body as he could.

"Sure I did. I swam over there last night and sank the stupid boat," I answered with a sarcastic edge that surprised me.

"You dumb twerp!" Bob yelled at me, his face red and swollen with rage. "You stupid, dumb, feeble-minded little twerp!"

For some reason, that word sounded funny and I guess I smirked a little. Although he was almost five years older and much taller and heavier than I was, there was an unspoken understanding between us—perhaps because of his bad arm—that we would never have a real fight. At least, I had that understanding, but at that moment I wondered if he had the same understanding. He sure was angry and looked as if he wanted to kill me. I saw that my smartass comment had become the focus for all of the rage and frustration about his trip and all it meant to him, so I decided to back off and leave the room before finding out how committed he was to non-violence. I couldn't entirely suppress the involuntary smirk on my face, although I did try because I knew it wasn't a very good idea, mostly because it might betray my secret pleasure at Bob's disaster. Now, he'd have to stay home with me and share the daily torture. I felt guilty even thinking that and hoped it didn't show.

He caught me by surprise on the front stairs as I was going up to my room. His strong hand grabbed my ankle through the thin wooden balusters of the staircase and pulled my leg out from under me. I didn't have time to break the fall and my head and right shoulder hit the stairs in front of me hard. I bounced down the stairs feet-first. When I hit the landing, Bob pounced on me, knocking out my wind, punching me everywhere with his good arm. I wriggled out from under him and crawled on all fours up the stairs as fast as I could with Bob punching me and pulling me back. Somehow I made it to the top of the stairs first and stood up. With Bob two steps below me and our eyes on the same level, I thought in a flash of kicking him in the stomach or hurling myself at his throat sending us crashing backwards down the stairs, which probably would have killed us both. Then, he reached out and clamped his powerful left hand around my neck and squeezed like he always did, which really hurt. He used to be able to hold me far enough away from his body this way so that my hands couldn't reach him, but I'd grown, and this time when I swung at him, I hit him in the stomach. He was stunned and let my neck go, but not for long, because he came back at me madder than ever, this time trying to hit me with his left hand and holding the bum one in front of him as a shield. I didn't want to hit his bad arm, so I waited for an opening, and when he swung with his mean left arm and missed me, I punched him again hard in the stomach. He couldn't believe it and, to tell the truth, neither could I. I'd surprised him. I could see it in his eyes. I could also see that he was getting truly mad now, mad that his little brother had actually punched him. I began to worry that my new ability would desert me and he'd beat the hell out of me. So, I began to retreat. I backed up until we were on the steep, slippery wooden stairs to the third-floor attic. I didn't have a plan about what I'd do when I got up there. I was a cornered animal, retreating but not knowing where I was going. Bob was still flailing out at me, hitting me often enough so that I was hurting, still trying to tackle me on the stairs. He was red in the face and his eyes were on fire. I was scared when we got to the top. There wasn't anywhere to go. The doors off the hall in the attic were either locked or had been stuck for ages or went to closets full of dusty old clothes and suitcases.

I got to the top of the stairs first and had a moment to catch my breath before Bob got all the way up. Then, he was standing there, seemingly about two feet taller than me, looking down like a homicidal maniac about to strike. He rushed at me and we grappled and wrestled and fell to the floor. He got up quickly and yelled at me: "Damn you, fight!" I had punched him—only twice, mostly because I was always going backwards or up the stairs trying to get out of the way of that dangerous sledgehammer left hand, but also because I just didn't want to hit him again. I wanted him to stop hitting me. When he yelled at me and I didn't answer him and just stood there, he rushed me again, and again we went down grunting and twisting and wrestling on the floor, our clothes now rumpled and covered with chalky dust.

He tried to get my neck in that death grip, but I broke free with a spasm of energy and stood up. For an instant, Bob was on all fours looking up at me. I think he expected me to kick him, or at least do something to use my momentary advantage, but I didn't. He launched himself straight at me and the force sent us both to the edge of the steep, slippery stairs, very close to tumbling over. That did it for me. I felt a huge surge of desperate strength and, although I was under Bob, I threw him off me. I actually threw him off! He was stunned at that, but it seemed to fuel his rage even more, not stop him. As he picked himself up, getting ready to charge me again, I raised my right hand as if I was holding a hammer over my head. "Stop it," I said, crying and gasping. "For Christ's sake, stop it right now. If you don't, I'm going to hit you, and I don't want to hit you."

"So, go ahead and hit me, you little turd," he screamed. "Go ahead, I dare you."

"No," I shouted. "I won't."

"Why not?" he shrieked.

In a weirdly quiet voice, I answered, "I won't fight you." Then I yelled, "You're CRIPPLED!"

As that terrible word echoed around the attic, Bob froze with his left arm extended to grab me. I saw the fire in his eyes die. I saw him shrivel up inside and outside. He didn't move a single muscle but just looked straight at me. I saw the unthinking, unfeeling animal rage in his eyes change in an instant and melt into something else, something weak and vulnerable, as if he had just understood that, yes, he couldn't fight, and, yes, he was crippled, and cripples don't fight, and, yes, that was the way it was. His shoulders sagged as he turned and stumbled down the stairs. I saw Mom at the bottom as Bob passed her; she must have been there for several minutes. She looked up at me with horror and groaned: "My God! What have you done?"

It took a few days for things to return to normal between Bob and me, but they did. I never told him I was sorry and ashamed at what I said, although I was. I wanted to tell him what I said wasn't true at all—he wasn't really crippled, he was very strong and could fight pretty damn well. Why had I ever said something so stupid? I never asked him, and he never told me, what he felt about our fight. We just didn't talk about it at all, ever again. We did reach an uneasy truce, and the first time he asked me to get something for him, I did it gladly. I noticed that he was being uncommonly nice to me too, which I took to mean that he also wanted to patch things up. That was good because, for the rest of the summer, until he went off to Harvard, we needed to be allies if we were to survive the silent fog that separated our parents from each other and from us. What would I do when he left? He'd be gone for a whole school year. I couldn't get away until I went off to Exeter, and that was over a year away. I didn't think that I could last that long.

In September, Bob went off to Harvard and I went back to nearby Hackley, a private school in Tarrytown not far from Ardsley-on-Hudson where I was a day student, for the eighth grade. There, if you made High Honors, which was pretty tough, they gave you a holiday of a whole day; if you just made Honors—still good—it was half a day. I did well and had High Honors for the two marking periods that fall. Mom took me somewhere special on those two days. On one, we drove into New York City on the Saw Mill River Parkway and she took me to the Egyptian wing of the Metropolitan Museum. I had read Anne Terry White's *Lost Worlds*, about the Pharaohs and life in ancient Egypt, about five times, and I could have spent months in the Metropolitan looking at the mummies, the amazing hieroglyphs and the tomb they'd reconstructed right there, but we went on to the Museum of Natural History and saw the dinosaur bones and the show at the Hayden Planetarium. On the other Honors Day, just before the Christmas vacation, she took me to a play on Broadway, *New Faces of 1952*. When she bought the tickets, I don't think she had known much about it, because it had a few suggestive acts, including a very sexy Eartha Kitt slinking cat-like around and over a luxurious couch purring "Monotonous." Mom squirmed a bit and would have loved to leave at the intermission but, after all, this was my day and I was certainly enjoying myself, so she just toughed it out.

That night, she told Dad one of her "white" lies—that we'd spent the day visiting her sister, my Aunt Mary, who ran a consignment shop in the city called The Two Time Shop where she sold the once-worn, castoff dresses of rich women. Dad knew that Mom went to see Aunt Mary a lot, so he didn't ask any questions. On those days when we really did visit her, I sat around the shop while Mom and Aunt Mary talked, only getting interested when the subject was one of Aunt Mary's best customers, Mrs. Gary Cooper. Mom knew I was bored and we wouldn't stay too long. She'd make the day a little more special by taking me to Schrafft's restaurant and letting me order anything I wanted. She wouldn't order a drink.

Those days with Mom, at museums and even at Aunt Mary's shop, were wonderful. Mom was pretty and fun to be with and it was just the two of us. Since the Honor Days were regular school days for the other kids in my class, I felt as if we were playing hooky. It was as if we were doing something a little wrong and secret. I also remember Mom driving on the Saw Mill River Parkway, white knuckles gripping the steering wheel, putting her foot on the pedal, then the brake, on and off again, but still happy, with a smile on her face and her red hair in a sort of halo from the sun around her head. There was no fog around when I was alone with Mom. It came in the front door every night when Dad came home. My days with her were good days.

I had my first migraine on Thanksgiving Day that year, although I didn't know what it was then. It started before Bob and his new girlfriend Lynn Danforth and some of my uncles, aunts and cousins arrived for Thanksgiving dinner when spots appeared before my eyes as if I'd just looked straight into a flash bulb. I couldn't see anything for half an hour before the pounding headache began. I was pretty sure I had a brain tumor. Lynn came up to my room to see me and massaged my temples with a cold washcloth for a while. That felt pretty good, and it was nice to have her fussing over me, but the headache lasted for the rest of the day and got worse and worse until late in the afternoon. As it was getting dark, I got sick and threw up. Then I felt better, although my head felt like I'd gone a few rounds with the new heavyweight champ Rocky Marciano. I missed Thanksgiving dinner and my cousins and singing folk songs and show tunes with Mom at the piano, but I couldn't eat. I thought my brain would burst and I was going to die.

I wondered if the strange headache was self-inflicted—did I bring it on myself as punishment for something bad I'd done? I'd gotten caught smoking cigarettes—I'd taken one pack out of the carton of Phillip Morrises that Dad always kept in the top drawer of the chest in the living room where I'd found the old photographs of Mom and Dad. I'd taken the cigarettes outside to the back of our lawn behind some trees where I knew I couldn't be seen from the house. I smoked about ten cigarettes one after the other before getting sick to my stomach. Mom came home and found me vomiting and was worried that I was really sick until she noticed that I reeked of tobacco. But, while she was angry at me, it wasn't the end of the world, and I didn't think that was what was causing the headache. Maybe, it was God punishing me for any number of sinful things I'd thought about, like what it would be like to have sex with a beautiful girl—maybe, even Marilyn Monroe. But, I didn't get a headache every time I'd thought about sex—if I had, I would have had one continuous, never-ending headache. So, I probably had a brain tumor.

MOM PLAYED THE piano a lot. In the daytime, she would warm up with incredibly complex and difficult drills by Czerny or she'd sight-read Bach fugues. Sometimes she went to the home of another woman who gave piano lessons and played pieces for eight hands on two pianos with three other women, all of them accomplished pianists. At night, when friends were at our house, well after the point when her daytime character completely disappeared and my Night Mother emerged full-blown, she would play show tunes, both current and forgotten, endlessly, all by ear, and all executed with skill and accuracy. She loved those songs and loved nothing better than to be surrounded by lots of people singing the songs they loved; and, she could play them all. She wanted me to be able to play the piano and insisted that I take lessons, which I did. Since I liked playing by ear much more than reading the pieces my teacher assigned to me, she often listened to me picking songs out on the keyboard.

One day, she sat down next to me on the piano bench and told me that an ear for music ran in our family and I had a good ear. I'd inherited it just like my name, which was the name of Dad's mother's great uncle who had fought on the Union side in the Civil War. Mom then led me upstairs to the attic and rummaged around in the back of a dusty closet and came out with an old box that contained my namesake's family Bible that she said I would inherit someday. It had a beautifully embossed leather binding that was falling apart from sheer age. Its first few pages contained a record of the births, marriages and deaths of earlier generations entered in several different ornate scripts I couldn't read. She also showed me his old, rusted Civil War sword and said that it would be mine one day, as well. And then she took me to the beautiful, tall, drop-front maple desk in the front hall which she said he'd made with his own hands. She wanted to keep it until she died, then it too would become mine.

MOM AND DAD had a black tie New Year's Eve dinner party to welcome in 1953 with, maybe, twenty-five or thirty people. I stayed in my room out of the way with my door shut and went to bed before midnight but couldn't sleep because of all the noise. Well after midnight most everyone had left but Mom still wouldn't give up. I could hear her playing as the front door closed on the departing guests. I could also hear Mr. Kimball—who along with his wife, Bunny, and Ashley and Libby Thorndike formed the remaining hard core—mumbling, not singing, the words to the songs he knew in an off-key monotone. I could also hear Dad, who loved to sing the old songs, too, and encouraged Mom to keep playing, sometimes getting her drinks to keep her fueled. I was sure he was doing that right now. From the sound of his voice, I could tell he was happy. I also knew from how loud he was talking and singing that he had a real buzz on himself. Since I couldn't sleep, I got out of bed and went to the top of the stairs and looked down through the balusters. Mom's magic fingers began to play one of Dad's all-time favorites, which, I think, was called "Living in Arabian History." As Mom vamped the intro- duction, Dad hushed the others, wrapped something that looked like a woman's red silk scarf around his head—sheik-like—and danced and swooped around the living room croaking about the desert breezes and dancing girls of Araby: "Back in those days let me be dwelling," he sang. Maybe so.

Most people thought that hearing her play was a lot of fun, even when she was blitzed, and it truly was—to a point. The ending point for me was that this was my mother, not some amusing, drunken barroom slattern whose fingers could work magically although she was too drunk to speak.

THE REST OF my last year at Hackley went by very fast and I "graduated" from the Lower School in early June near the top of my class. I played left tackle on the Lower School football team— we had games against Buckley and Allen-Stevenson in the mud on Randall's Island. I was the pitcher on the baseball team, but

I really wanted to play first base, as my hero Gil Hodges did for the incomparable Brooklyn Dodgers.

Later, during the sweltering dog days of mid-August, Bob told me that he was feeling very depressed and pessimistic about the future. He said he just couldn't get excited about being at Harvard or anything else; he didn't care at all. He felt suffocated in the house—we both agreed on that—but he had this odd lack of desire to do anything about it. He wanted to get away someplace, he said, but there wasn't any place to go. He'd called two of his Exeter friends, angling for an invitation to visit one on Martha's Vineyard and the other on Squam Lake in New Hampshire. Neither had come through for different reasons, and Bob suspected that neither of them had really tried. He knew some other guys he could call, but he'd pretty much given up the idea and hadn't made any other calls. Instead, he'd tried to rev up some of his old enthusiasm for writing detective stories under his pseudonym of "St. John (which Bob pronounced 'Sinjin') Parker" which was a name that struck him as full of urbanity, intelligence and sly wit; I thought it was pretty wimpy and boring. Now Gil Hodges, the great Brooklyn Dodger first baseman —there was a name to reckon with; obviously a guy with a name like that was smart and big and strong. "Sinjin" Parker had to have loose wrists and wear ascots and velvet slippers.

Bob spent a lot of time on the third-floor of our house arranging one of the empty rooms into suitable quarters for an urbane, intelligent and slyly witty writer of detective stories. After unpacking his suitcase and stowing it, he had put the armchair in his bedroom up there with his desk, a floor lamp and a little hooked rug he found in the cellar. He'd sit up there for hours, sometimes pecking with one finger at his Smith-Corona, but mostly practicing the signature of "St. John Parker" until it looked right. He filled up a couple of spiral notebooks with nothing but that signature. I don't think he really wrote much of anything else that summer.

One night quite late, after about two weeks of writing signatures, as he was lying in bed in his room next to mine with the door between open to let the hot, muggy August air circulate better, Bob asked me quietly in the dark if I was still awake.

"Yes. At least I am now."

"What are you going to do with your life, anyway?"

"How 'bout we talk about it in the morning? I'm half asleep and can't deal with such a jejune topic," I'd answered groggily using my big deal word for the week I had to learn for Exeter.

"Hey, I'm serious; I'd like to know if you've thought about it. I've been thinking a lot about it and I can't see myself doing anything with my life. Don't you ever feel that way?"

"You mean that you don't know if you want to be a lawyer or a doctor or something like that? I don't know that either. Don't you think you'll find something you're interested in at college?"

"That's just it. I think I know, lying right here, that I will never, ever find anything that I want to do. I will plod through life always doing something I don't want to do just because I have to do something. I just know I'll never do anything I want to do because there is no such thing. It's just not worth it."

"What do you mean 'it's not worth it'?" I asked.

"Plodding through life like that. If I know—and I mean I'm absolutely positive—that life will always be one long let-down, why do it? Why go through that? Why not just end it?"

"Jeez, Bob, what are you saying? How can you be so sure? I mean things can't be that bad, and how can you be so sure you won't feel differently when you're back at Harvard?"

"I just know, that's all. I am absolutely certain. I can't explain it, but it's true. Do you know what I mean?"

"I dunno. Maybe. I've had a feeling that I knew something like that, but couldn't explain it. I still think it can change. I know if I felt the way you say you do, I'd be pretty depressed too. In fact, just thinking about how you feel makes me depressed. I mean it's enough just living here, but that's too much," I said. "You're not going to do anything are you?"

There was a long silence as we both lay there wide-awake in the dark, sweltering in the breathless August heat. "Hey, Bob," I called after awhile, "you're not really thinking of doing something, are you?"

"Maybe. I think I'll give it another week and unless something changes, which I doubt, I think I will do something about it."

"Jeez, Bob! What?"

"You mean how? I don't know yet. Whatever it is won't be messy or violent or anything. Pills maybe, or maybe I'll put my head in the oven and turn the gas on when nobody's around. I don't know. I haven't figured that part out yet."

I didn't say anything and just tossed around in bed thinking. Here was my own brother talking about actually committing suicide and I'm not even in there trying to talk him out of it. What kind of a wimp am I? What would I do without Bob? I'd miss him too much. He just can't do it! I'd be all alone in that house. I sure don't want that to happen. My hands were cold and clammy.

I imagined Dad and Mom, dressed in black, weeping as Bob's coffin was lowered into a freshly dug grave on a green hillside overlooking the gray Hudson River in a torrential downpour. Then, the three of us would get into a long, black Cadillac limousine and ride home, sobbing, saying nothing.

"If you do it, I'll do it too," I said breaking the silence.

"Why?" asked Bob, surprised.

"Some of the same reasons you have and some of my own, I guess. I couldn't stand living here alone," I said, wanting to add that "alone" meant without him, without Bob, but I couldn't say that. And, anyhow, even as depressed as I was about everything, I knew down deep that I was just saying this to Bob and that I wouldn't really do it.

I'd hoped that if I went along with him by saying we both were going to do ourselves in, he'd change his mind about it. But, it didn't actually happen that way. Instead, the next day and the next, Bob made several references to our "suicide pact." He'd say things like "shall we take a last walk to so-and-so's house?" or "do you realize that we'll never see snow again?" Bob was actually operating on the basis that his life would soon end. His spirits improved a great deal, and he showed great interest in things he'd never bothered with before, like flowers and birds and trees. To him, the end was very real.

As the summer crawled by, I began to think that Bob might actually do it. He still thought we were in this thing together, but I was trying desperately to think of some way to stop him, or some reason for him to change his mind about it. I didn't come up with any clever plan, and the clock kept ticking.

One morning in August, I was reading in the *New York Herald*

Tribune about how the Brooklyn Dodgers had beaten the Giants the day before and Gil Hodges had hit his 25th home run—he was having a great year and it looked like Brooklyn was going to win the National League pennant—when Bob bounced downstairs and joined me at the dining room table. He was in a better mood than I'd seen him in all summer long. All that morning, he was positively jovial, jumping all around the house in high spirits. I didn't feel too sure of what was going to happen and was too nervous to feel good because I thought this might be The Day. It seemed silly when the stakes were so huge, but I didn't know how to tell Bob that I'd changed my mind and was not going on this particular trip with him; I'd made up my mind to keep living even if he wasn't around. I wanted to tell him that all kinds of people would miss him, Mom and Dad, all his friends, and even me too—if I had to go that far—and that I really wished he wouldn't do it. If that didn't work, I'd get mad and say that I was going to tell Mom and Dad and they'd lock him up in a padded cell somewhere so he couldn't do it. I'd shout and scream and carry on, but I also thought that if he was really going to do it, no one could stop him, and that made me very sad—so sad that I began to think that I'd do it too, after all.

Lang Stevenson, Bob's best friend, showed up at our house in the early afternoon that day, which almost always meant trouble for me. Whenever Lang and Bob got together, I was usually either excluded or, more often, they thought of things to do to me which they thought were funny and I didn't. Sadists. So, I decided to go up to my room, out of their way, and try to figure out something to stop Bob. I didn't know how much time I had left.

"Hey, Bumppo," I heard Lang shout from downstairs after a

while. "Come on down here for a minute; there's something we want to show you." Lang had called me "Bumppo" ever since my cousin Sherry dubbed me "Natty Bumppo" when I was a toddler leading her around the mysteries of the garden in our back yard in Ardsley like James Fenimore Cooper's *Pathfinder*, and it stuck.

There was a tone in Lang's voice that gave me a creepy feeling that something not altogether good for me was up, but being incredibly gullible, I wondered if maybe this was one of those rare times when they did have something interesting to see, like a sex book or something. Once, Lang had showed us the most terrific sex book I'd ever seen, *The Way of a Man with a Maid*, which he supposedly borrowed from what Lang said was his father's "secret library of the world's greatest pornography" kept strictly under lock and key.

I decided to risk it and went downstairs to see what Lang had up his sleeve. Bob and Lang were in our big, pine-paneled living room, which was usually off-limits to Bob and me. This was a good sign. What could they possibly do to me in there? Still, I opened the door warily and, not seeing anybody, gingerly stepped in.

Bob and Lang were hiding behind the door and when I got far enough inside the room, they jumped me and started whopping me with pillows from the couch. At first, they were both yelling and laughing with great amusement at my attempts to cover my face and save my glasses from being destroyed. I took a glancing blow on the side of my head and my glasses flew off and sailed straight into the wall. The frame broke in the middle and came to rest in two pieces on the floor. They stopped hitting me.

"Jeez, you jerks. That isn't funny at all! Goddammit, that was my only pair of frigging glasses, you frigging idiots!" I screamed in rage at the two fuzzy outlines of Bob and Lang. I grabbed the nearest object I could see, which was a wooden, armless side chair in the corner of the room, picked it up and threw it at Bob. He wasn't expecting that, and it caught him on his shoulder and the side of his head, stunning him for a second. When Lang saw that, he jumped on me.

"You little asshole," he hissed, suddenly enraged, as he knocked me down on my back. He sat on my chest and pinned my arms to the floor. "We're going to teach you something you'll never forget."

Bob recovered, picked up one of the pillows and mashed it down over my face despite my thrashing around. I couldn't breathe, and my yells were muffled so much that even I couldn't hear them, just little grunts that didn't seem serious. I was losing consciousness and knew that I had only a few seconds to get free or I was going to take the Big Trip before Bob. With one great spasm of energy, I kicked and twisted my whole body with enough force to wind up on my stomach, free of the lethal pillow. I gagged and gulped for air, unable to speak.

Bob and Lang were standing watching me when I finally stood up, trembling and shivering. Lang had a little smirk on his face. He seemed pleased that he had, indeed, taught me a lesson I'd never forget. Bob's face was different. There was something in his face far beyond the gloating of a bully. He wasn't smiling at all. Even without my glasses, I could see a crazed look of pure, savage hatred in his hard eyes. My brother, Bob, the only person in the world I thought I could trust, who alone also knew the daily hell of that poisonous house, whose life I cared about more than anything else in the world—Bob really wanted to hurt me and, maybe, even kill me.

I ran out of the living room, through the hall and the dining room, and stopped to catch my breath in the small pantry next to the kitchen.

"Maybe we should go after him," I heard Lang say. "He looked a little shook up."

"No," Bob answered. "Let him sulk." His voice was flat.

I tried to picture what Bob was doing at that moment. Was he sitting, slumped down? Did he look sad? Did he feel sorry? Did he feel anything? Did he know how he'd looked at me? Had he just lost control for a second and now regretted it terribly? I tried, but just couldn't get a picture of him in my mind; the words I'd heard told me nothing. What was that horrific look in his eyes? For a terrible moment, an image of myself, much younger and smaller, popped into my mind. I was sitting in Mom's lap. She was drooling drunk and her eyes didn't focus. Her head was bobbing up and down as though she was about to fall asleep. She hugged me too tightly and called me her "only whole child"—while Bob was staring at us. I shuddered. Even the memory made me want to throw up. Was she entirely insane when she got drunk? How could she even have thought that? Maybe Bob did hate me.

I went into the kitchen and closed the back door and the one window that was half-open. We had an old gas stove that was as old as the house and had no pilot light which meant you had to light it with a match after the gas was turned on. Mom was afraid of it.

I turned the gas on, opened the oven door, and sat down cross-legged in front of it. I listened to the hiss of the gas, and asked myself what in blazes was I doing, for it was very clear to me at that moment that, although I was hurt and scared and confused by the look in Bob's eyes, I had no intention whatsoever of doing myself in. I was positive that Bob and Lang would come looking for me soon and find me and be very sorry for what they'd done to me. Boy, would they be sorry! I'd get out of it by making some dumb joke about how I was just waiting for Bob to follow through with his end of our bargain, hoping that, with Lang there, Bob would be embarrassed out of his skull and, maybe, see how stupid his plan was. As the minutes passed, I got a little worried about them searching for me, but still thought they'd find me soon enough.

The next thing I remember is Lang picking me up by the arms. Bob was running around opening the kitchen door and all the windows. Both of them were yelling orders at each other. Get him outside! Walk him around! Get some fresh air in here! Don't make any sparks, for Christ's sake! Keep him on his feet! I couldn't tell who was saying what, only that the whole world seemed very soft and fuzzy without my glasses and very sweet and pleasant. It seemed strange that Bob and Lang were in a dither when everything was so nice and calm.

Lang took me outside and walked me around our backyard, holding me up with his arm around my waist until I could walk myself. I felt like throwing up and got a terrific headache.

"What in the world did you think you were doing, slugger?" Lang asked me intensely and with real concern. "Nothing could be that bad."

How to explain that things were not as they appeared, that I wasn't really going to do it, that I knew they'd find me, and that what I'd done was just a really bad joke—a stupid ploy to stop my brother from killing himself? At that moment, as it dawned on me how close I'd come, I wasn't sure I believed that explanation either. It just didn't make a lot of sense.

Bob did blame himself. He thought I'd decided to follow through on our crazy suicide pact and berated himself for ever having thought of such a stupid idea. He said he had never, ever taken the plan seriously. He said he thought that, in all our discussions about it, I was just being a good guy and humoring him when he was down. For some reason, it had made him feel better to pretend that he was going to do it. It broke the monotony and let him think that he wasn't going to have to put up with existing in our house forever. He'd never thought I'd take him seriously. Anyway, I wasn't sure he was telling the truth but I knew that I couldn't explain what I was really doing either.

Bob and I were in better spirits for the rest of the summer, which was almost over at that point, me getting ready to go off to Exeter and Bob back to Harvard. Gil Hodges was doing great, and the Dodgers were fighting for the National League pennant. Bob promised me that he would never tell Mom and Dad about what had happened. He also made me promise that as soon as I got to Exeter I would go and see Dr. Heyl, the school psychiatrist who had helped some of his friends, and I did promise. In fact, Bob called and made an appointment for me with Dr. Heyl during the first week of school. I wasn't sure what I was going to tell him.

Chapter Three

I TOOK MY second trip up to Exeter in September 1953. It seemed to take a lot longer than it had for Bob's graduation, maybe because I wasn't very excited about starting out at this place I'd seen only once before. Dad drove, of course. He never let Mom drive when he was in the car. He said she made him nervous, which was fine with me since her driving made me nervous, too. I tried not to think about what Exeter was going to be like. I was going there no matter what, so worrying about it didn't seem worthwhile. When we finally got there, Mom and Dad helped me unload my suitcase and some other things onto the pavement outside Dunbar Hall, the freshman dorm I'd been assigned to.

"You know I've got to get back tonight," said Dad, "so we can't stay." He said goodbye to me and Mom hugged me and said she wished they could stay, but said "you know your father..." and they drove off to go right back home. It happened so fast. I knew they weren't going to stay very long but, all of a sudden, there I was, alone, standing in front of the dorm with my suitcase, my Webcor record player, some 45 RPM records, a reading lamp and some books I wanted to have with me all in a big box I could hardly carry. Couldn't they have stayed long enough to take a peek at my room and help me lug my stuff up there?

I looked around. Had Bob lived in Dunbar during his first year at Exeter? I wasn't sure, but I remembered parading with Dad and his classmates past its ivy-covered brick walls and its twin, Webster Hall, planted right next to it. In front of Dunbar, across a wide lawn with an enormous tree—maybe, an elm, but I wasn't very good at the names of trees—I saw an old white house with columns in front and, behind it, a Georgian brick building that I remembered was the library. Across the street that divided Dunbar, Webster, the white house and the library from the main part of the campus, I could see the Academy Building and a church on its left—the only smudge of gray stone among the green trees, the white houses and the red brick, ivy-covered buildings. It all looked familiar but, at the same time, it was very new and strange. Maybe I'd seen those buildings before but I didn't know what went on inside them or how this huge place worked. It was one thing to parade around these buildings behind a big drum but it was quite another thing to think that I'd be spending the next four years here and would have to get to know them inside and out.

How could they just drive off? I didn't even know where I was supposed to eat. Another boy who was watching us unload asked if the people he saw with me were my parents, "Yes" I said.

"Do they live in the City? I saw the New York plates."

"Just outside the City."

"Oh. I live in the City. My parents just left, too. What's your name?"

I didn't answer. I didn't feel like talking to anyone. I didn't want to stay at Exeter. I wanted to go back home, but here I was and here it looked as if I was going to stay. So, after the boy who was trying to talk to me gave up, I wrestled my suitcase and the big box into the dorm, found my name on a room assignment list posted on a bulletin board and lugged everything up to my room on the second floor, planning to brood a little. There was also a notice on the bulletin board saying that all new Juniors—called "Preps" by everyone—should go to an assembly in the Academy Building at four o'clock that afternoon. Bob had made an appointment for me at five o'clock with Dr. Heyl, the school shrink, and I'd promised him I'd go. I didn't want to, but Bob said Dr. Heyl had seemed to help a couple of his friends and so I had nothing to lose. Maybe, I'd learn something.

I'D BEEN GIVEN a single room—whether because of my father, brother, uncles and cousins who had come here before me or by the luck of the draw, I didn't know. It was pretty big and pleasant, with bare wood floors and clean white walls smelling a little of fresh paint. There was a metal frame bed with a gray wool blanket and a wooden desk and chair. The single window looked out on some big trees in the back of the building, so I'd probably be able to sneak a cigarette hanging out of it without being seen. I was glad that I wouldn't have to deal with living in the same room with another person, something I'd never done before and worried about as the summer was ending. Bob had become good friends with all his roommates at Exeter, but I was sure that I wouldn't be so lucky. I thought I'd probably get some scrawny brain who studied all the time or a budding campus politician who'd see his big chance to brownnose the faculty by busting his own roommate for smoking.

After I'd unpacked the essentials—that is, my Webcor and stack of 45 RPM records—I left my room to go to the assembly for new kids in the Academy Building. I walked alone but next to a group of my new classmates going the same way. The boy who had tried to talk to me when my parents left caught up to me. I was looking at the pavement in front of me pretending not to notice him as we walked but I couldn't help being dazzled by his gleaming new white bucks, which were almost phosphorescent in the evening sunlight. Now, even I knew—from Bob, I guess—that no one ever wore new white bucks. They had to have dirt rubbed into them and then they should be bent, twisted and thrown around a lot. Only when they were just about falling apart could they be worn.

So, here was a boy from New York City who was actually wearing brand new, gleaming white bucks. Maybe, I thought, at least some City kids weren't as savvy as I'd heard, which was a lot. They were supposed to be very smooth and sophisticated and know a lot about girls and drinking, all of which made me unsure about how to handle them. I decided that, if I didn't say much, they'd think I knew something about those things too, which I didn't. So, since this boy was from the City—even if he didn't know about white bucks—I didn't say anything.

As we ambled along together in silence, I could feel his need to talk bubbling up like water about to boil. I took my eyes off his luminous shoes and glanced up at his crisp, creased khakis (another mistake: no wrinkles), his pink and white striped button-down shirt (okay, pretty good) and his pink and blue tie and blue blazer with gold buttons. He looked altogether like a back-to-prep school mannequin at Brooks Brothers, as if his mother had bought the whole ensemble for him not realizing that no real person was supposed to dress like that. Maybe City kids didn't know some things, after all, I thought. The pressure to say something became too much for him.

"What do you know about this stupid assembly we have to go to, anyway?" he blurted, pretending to be utterly bored.

"Not much," I mumbled. "I hope they tell us where to eat."

"Good point," he said enthusiastically, hoping the conversation might lead somewhere, but it didn't. We continued along, staring at the pavement, or in my case, his shoes. After some time, he tried again.

"So you're not from the City, ah, New York City, that is?"

"No, a little north. Ardsley-on-Hudson. It's up in Westchester, about twenty miles from the City." I was embarrassed by the hyphens and how pseudo-English "Ardsley-on-Hudson" sounded.

"I guess you told me that," he said, although I hadn't. "Anyway, I was pretty sure I knew everyone here who comes from the City." I hoped he was lying, thinking of the swarms of City kids who were on the class roster I'd received about three weeks before and how cliquish they were supposed to be.

"No kidding?" I offered, hoping that the tiny ember of our conversation might die.

"Well, maybe not all of them. Anyway, my name's Peter

Bradford. What's yours? I've lived in the City all my life. I went to St. Bernard's. God, am I glad to get out of there! I did like some things there, of course, and I liked living at home. I don't know how I'm going to like that part—living up here, I mean. How do you feel about it? Not living at home, I mean. Well, there's still the summer, I guess. God, I had a great summer on Nantucket. Where do you go? I mean, do you go anywhere? I guess I'm lucky. We have a house on Nantucket and I've always gone there for the summer for as long as I can remember. It looks over the cliffs down to the beach, at the far end of the island. There's not much there; that's what my parents like about it, I guess. Sometimes I wish there was a little more going on, but then one can always import entertainment, can't one? Only I don't do that too much. The whole point is relaxing, isn't it, and if you do too much, you lose the point. Right? Anyway, that's how my parents see it and I can sure see their point. Boy, did I need a vacation this summer. And my father, he needed one worse. He's a writer. What does your father do?" I wondered if I'd have a chance to get a word in before I learned everything there was to know about him.

"He's a lawyer. He works at a big law firm in the City and commutes on the train every day. I don't see too much of him." I felt uncomfortable revealing so much.

"Yeah, boy, do I know about that. My old man keeps saying he's going to take me striper fishing or to play golf or something, and it never happens. I mean, never, not even on Nantucket where all he seems to do is loaf around. He sure is into relaxing. Anyway, I don't need him for action. Right?"

The Academy Building loomed up before us and we found

ourselves pressed into the noisy crowd squeezing up the outside
steps, through the front door into the big hallway and flowing
up both of its two wide white marble staircases to the Assembly
Hall on the second floor. The flow took him up the staircase on
one side of the building and me the other. He was taller than
most of the others, as was I, so we could see each other for a
while as we were swept apart.

"See you later?" he called out, almost plaintively. "Say, what
was your name?" He looked a little confused, as if he wasn't sure
whether I'd told him or not, which I hadn't. I sure wasn't going
to shout it out there, so I pretended I couldn't hear him with all
the noise and just shrugged my shoulders, looking helplessly at
him as the tide carried us into the Assembly Room.

WE WERE IN a giant room with a raised stage at the far end
where a teacher and some older boys, probably seniors, were sitting waiting their turns at the lectern to tell us what's what. All
the new boys were sitting in rows of black wooden benches in al-
phabetically assigned seats facing the stage. Peter Bradford was
a couple of seats away, on my right. The room reminded me of a
church but there were no crosses or any other religious symbols
I could see.

A small, thin-faced senior with an almost-bald crew cut, thick,
clear plastic glasses and ears that stuck out went to the lectern. I
listened for a moment, as he told us that working for *The Exonian*,
which was the "oldest prep school newspaper in America," was
so rewarding and worthwhile even if it did make it hard to find
the time to do all the reading and other homework we'd have. So,
not wanting to think of homework, I tuned him out and looked

back up at the dark, glaring portraits of old, unsmiling men on the wall. I knew I didn't belong in this place. I didn't want to be like them. I even felt depressed at the idea that maybe some of the other kids sitting right there around me actually wanted to hang up there someday. The truth is that I could hardly bear sitting in that room at all with all those eager faces around me, just waiting to hit the books and get on with it, and all those old farts on the wall nodding, yes, work very hard, be very good and one day you too may join us.

It's not that I wasn't willing to work hard. I just didn't know why I should. Bob hadn't worked very hard and seemed proud of having "greased" his way into Harvard. I assumed I'd do that too, and so getting into Harvard wasn't a big deal—that would happen naturally. So, what was the point of studying things like Latin and Algebra that seemed totally useless? Of course, I knew that I had to go to school somewhere for the next four years and, maybe, Exeter was better than most. Deep down, though, I knew that what I felt didn't really matter at all; Exeter was just something I had to go through. Almost everyone else in my family had. Dad told me he'd registered me at Exeter only days after I was born and never considered sending me anywhere else and, yes, he felt the same way about Bob and me going to Harvard. That didn't bother me—Exeter and Harvard would be part of my life like my one tweed jacket that Bob had worn before me. Now it was my turn.

The sound of a baritone adult voice startled me and my wandering mind bolted back to my seat in the Assembly Room. At the lectern stood a bald man with rimless glasses and a bow tie. He gripped the lectern with both of his hands as if he was about to lift it up over his head and throw it at us if we got out of line. He got my attention.

He started out by saying that his name was Phillips Wilson— Mr. Wilson to us, he made clear—and that he was an English teacher and the master of Webster Hall, the other dorm reserved for Preps. Big deal, I thought. He talked about all the dorm rules and regulations, lights out, smoking only in the buttrooms for kids over fourteen who had written permission (which left me out on both counts), no excessive noise tolerated, and so on. I was starting to drift back to the portraits on the wall when he suddenly finished. Then, a hugely tall and skinny senior with horn-rimmed glasses, gray flannels, a terrific brown tweed jacket and really shiny loafers took over at the lectern and told us that he was the President of the Student Council. He said that everyone at Exeter was there to help us. "Fat chance," I heard myself whisper to no one in particular. There was a lot of enthusiastic applause from the eager beavers around me when he finished, and then we all filed out of the room.

I had to get something to eat or I'd starve and it was so late that I'd never be able to find Dr. Heyl's house at the edge of the campus somewhere and keep the appointment Bob had made for me. I wasn't too disappointed about that, really, but I knew I couldn't get out of seeing him altogether. I decided to see if my new friend Peter Bradford had any ideas about eating. Maybe he'd listened better than I had.

I found Peter in the flow outside the Academy Building. Actually, I found his white bucks—they glowed in the gloom of the late afternoon. So I followed the glow at a distance and they took me, and a whole bunch of other kids, piling down some steps into a cafeteria called The Grill where everyone was yelling for something called "peanut-betweens"—toasted peanut butter and mayonnaise sandwiches, I found out soon enough—and pushing. I got in some kind of a line and waited forever to get a burger and a milkshake. Eating at Exeter wasn't going to be the easiest thing in the world.

DURING THE FIRST week at school, I discovered a nook in the library—it was called Davis Library—where I could read and blot out the whole world. I also discovered that holing up in my room doing a lot of homework in French, Latin, Ancient History and Algebra was no fun at all and meant I couldn't read as much as I wanted to. I also realized that anybody who even tried to do all that work wouldn't have time for anything else at all. Worse, the kids who did all that work were greasy grinds—misfits who were meant to stay in their rooms studying something or doing weird science things and were constantly made aware, in a thousand ways, by the other boys and even a lot of the teachers, that, despite their ability to get high marks, Exeter valued other things more highly, whatever our parents were told.

So, it was obvious that hanging around with any of the grinds would be about the biggest mistake I could make. They were untouchables. They tainted everyone who hung around them. Jocks weren't a whole lot better off. Everyone in the school cheered madly for the football and soccer stars when they won a game or did something amazing, but otherwise it was clear that such triumphs, and sports in general, weren't the most important things in the world. In fact, when the cheering stopped, being a big jock wasn't that great at all. Some had animal nicknames like "Bear" or "Beast" or "Turtle"—one was just called "Animal" and another "Woof"—and everybody assumed they were dumb, even if they weren't. Clearly, other things were of greater value to Exeter than athletic success.

If Exeter dumped on the brains and jocks, what did work became something of a puzzle, but I had to find some way that worked, at least for me. Maybe, I should just put in my time, as Bob did, get "Gentleman's C's," and move on to Harvard as he did.

Without thinking about it, I slowly became part of a loose bunch of five other Preps who lived in my dorm and seemed easy to get along with. They were quite different from each other and didn't fit into neat categories. Seth Bingham and Peter Bradford were a little preppy, but didn't overdo it. Bradford had begun to shape up a little and became more normal as the year went on. In fact, it didn't take too long for him to beat up his white bucks and otherwise begin to look as grubby as the rest of us, although we could tell that it was hard for him. He really wanted to be neater and cleaner than we considered totally acceptable. His roommate, Booger Baxter, was never neat and clean and probably had a lot to do with loosening up Bradford's standards. Seth Bingham was like Bradford; he just couldn't give up his Brooks Brothers penny loafers (without pennies) that he shined all the time. He was from Greenwich, Connecticut; I thought maybe that explained it. Bingham was also brilliant and could have been at the head of our class if he tried. Larry Fraser was a big, smart clod and an outstanding athlete; he'd gone to public school in Riverside, Connecticut, and had a football scholarship. The last of my gang, and a bit of an outsider, was Bob Downey.

He truly believed rules, and most laws, were made to be broken. He was content to squeak by and avoid the extremes of either being too good or too bad at anything, although he was really good at not being caught screwing up. In class, Downey always tried to be invisible, trying to sit somewhere he might not be noticed, which wasn't easy around an elongated oval table, with one hand over his mouth and eyes, hiding his perpetual sardonic smirk. Spending a lot of time with Downey made a lot of guys nervous about what he did, and also about what he didn't do, which was a lot of homework.

Larry Fraser became my best friend during the middle of the year. He'd spent the fall playing football ferociously, not doing all his homework because he was too tired to study. Since he didn't know anyone except other football players that first term, it was only after the football season was well over that he discovered that his hard work and growing prowess on the football field meant less than nothing afterwards. Nobody even remembered, or admitted they did. Larry returned from the battle only to find that nobody cared. He should have been doing something else.

Well, I cared, I must admit. Even before I got to know him well, I'd thought it was absolutely great that one of my own classmates had such amazing talent and dedication. I watched him play on Saturdays. He was easy to pick out because he was a lot taller than almost all of the other guys. He was also really good. An artist. I've always felt really good when someone does a particular thing so well or with such amazing skill and grace that it transforms that thing, whatever it is, into something important and beautiful. Watching Larry catch passes—he played right end on what Exeter called the "Big Green Team," equivalent, I think, to junior varsity other places—was like that. He was way oversized at about six feet three and a hundred and sixty pounds when he played that fall at the age of fourteen. He stuck out of the line like a tree among shrubs. His calves were the size of my thighs—the strongest legs I'd ever seen—and his head was too big for the helmet they gave him. At first, he was nothing less than awkward and ungainly, although I'd bet he shocked the other teams when they first saw him because he was so huge and wore big, shiny braces on his teeth, which he hated, but which made him look vicious.

In the beginning of the season, he wasn't a real threat to the enemy at all since his enormous tree-legs often tripped him up. He worked like a dog every minute of practice and, whenever he had some time to spare, he'd lift weights to strengthen his scrawny upper body and run patterns by himself against imaginary blockers and practice leaping for the ball. By the end of the season, he would float, as delicately as a ballet dancer, down the sidelines, obliterating blockers as if they weren't there, concentrating only on getting to the place the quarterback expected him to be. He'd glance over his shoulder to see the ball spiraling high in the air towards him, but sometimes it had been thrown too high for any normal receiver to reach. Then the magic would happen: he'd launch himself into the air like a huge bird taking off. You could feel the immense power of that launch and could only watch transfixed as he'd reach an amazing height, his toes pointed to the earth far beneath, and, with his arms fully extended way above his head and his eyes on the heavens, he'd just barely touch the ball with the tips of his outstretched fingers as it came high over his shoulder, but he'd hold onto it and float to earth with his prize. A miracle had occurred. Small, perhaps, but in my world miracles of any size didn't happen all that often.

While Larry usually had a startled "gee-whiz" expression on his face and found everything at Exeter new and interesting, Downey was sarcastic and sneered at everything and everybody, always ready with something bad to say about somebody, usually a teacher. He'd been away from home at one boarding school or another since he was six years old and had been expelled from several schools before he came to Exeter—from which he was also destined to get bounced, the only question being when. He thought he knew exactly how the world worked and was bitterly cynical—especially of the motives of all adults, and particularly politicians, parents and faculty adults. A lot of people didn't like him, maybe because of his perpetual smirk or because he could pick out anybody's weak spots, and make fun of them. He tried kidding Larry about the big, shiny braces on his teeth with bone-threatening results, so he took to doing safe things like rattling the fat kids in our class who hadn't matured a lot and were very lonely that year. He was also always looking out for things I'd never even think of—like a teacher's secret drinking or a faculty wife's cheating. He had a nose for such things. I don't know if everything he told us was true, but maybe it was. And, maybe, I was just too gullible.

"Of course they drink and fuck," he said. "What else do you expect them to do up here in this godforsaken place, play pocket pool all the time like us?" What was most amazing was that Downey thought of them just as ordinary people with all the usual imperfections. I didn't know any teachers and didn't think

I'd ever get to know any; they were another species. Who really knew what made them tick?

Downey had an explanation for everything. He was sure he would have had the highest grades at Exeter if he didn't masturbate so much. Also, he once explained to Larry that, certainly, football players were degraded at Exeter—the old farts on the faculty who couldn't do anything more strenuous except maybe move a chessman every half hour couldn't possibly admit that there was anything good about something none of them was ever able to do. It made perfect sense to him.

Booger Baxter—no one ever used his real name, which was Rodney—was something else. He was a tough, street-smart scholarship kid with wild hair and a broken front tooth who'd fought his way through public school in Brockton, Massachusetts—Rocky Marciano's hometown. He had no use whatever for Exeter or its mysterious dress code. We often had to spruce him up a bit, particularly if he was going to be seen by parents or other adults. He wore the same clothes every day—he never changed anything at all until he himself couldn't stand it anymore. That sometimes took weeks. And, he wore sneakers, not the low white tennis shoes that some guys thought looked pretty swish, but Keds, the high-topped kind with black canvas uppers and white rubber soles. He wore them everywhere, and one night, going up to the Eagle's Nest, they saved his life.

SOMEONE, PROBABLY DOWNEY, found a way to climb out of the dormer window of Booger's room on the fourth floor of Dunbar Hall. By holding on to the edge of the roof, and inching very carefully up the old slate shingles at a very steep angle, we could reach a fairly wide and long, flat, rectangular area depressed into the roof between Dunbar's two huge brick chimneys. No one sitting in the depression could be seen, since, looking up from the ground, the slate roof seemed uniform and sharply peaked. This secret place became our "Eagle's Nest"—our hideout, clubhouse and refuge. On sunny days, even in late autumn, we could use it comfortably, since it was protected from the wind and warmed by the chimney, but we also used it as the fall wore on and it got very cold and climbing up to it was more than normally life threatening. There was an exhilaration to know that we were in a place that was exclusively ours, known only to those we wanted to know, safe from any intrusion whatsoever.

At night in winter, I could look over the snow-covered campus for miles, the Georgian brick classroom buildings and dormitories arranged in neat little toy train-set blocks, the street lights winking all around the little town with its many white clapboard houses nestled in the snow with the inky-black ribbon of the still-flowing Squamscott River beyond.

Sometimes, being up in the Nest gave me a feeling of peace and warmth and contentment. I was safe and truly belonged to this place in the universe, this cozy, benign little world spread out below me. Other times when I was up there, everything seemed cold and bleak and remote and left me feeling lonely and isolated. Yet, I kept going up there, hoping for the good feelings and, if they didn't come, at least I could smoke without fear of getting caught.

One very cold day in early December, we all spent a few hours outdoors and then went back to our rooms in Dunbar to warm the chill out of our bones. On the way in, Booger said he was going up to the Eagle's Nest for a smoke. I said it was too cold. Bradford didn't say anything, but just followed Booger, leaving me trying to warm up with Larry, Seth and Downey who also weren't keen on going up to the Nest just then either. We sat around in the Dunbar common room for a while not saying much until Larry announced he was hungry, which he always was, unless at that moment he was already eating. He proposed that we all go to the Grill to get something to eat, which sounded good to the rest of us—at least it was a warm something to do—and we all walked out of the dorm together.

Larry was the first one to look up at the roof. He grabbed my shoulder with one hand and pointed upwards with the other…"Lookit that, Bumppo. Holy shit, it's Booger!" He almost whispered.

Booger was lying flat on his stomach, spread-eagled on the sharply sloping roof. His head was turned to the left and his fingers were spread wide apart grasping the cold, gray slate shingles. Since his back was to us, we couldn't see the expression on his face but could easily guess that he was scared to death since his feet were only inches from the green copper gutters at the edge of the roof and we all knew that a lot of that old slate could break off easily. Booger must have slipped going up to the Nest and slid sideways, feet first, down toward the edge of the roof. Somehow, he was able to stop himself just in time. He wasn't moving a muscle.

Bradford ran out of the dorm, panting. "Booger slipped! Christ, you guys, Booger slipped! Look at him up there. He's way out of reach and says he can't move. His fingers are all numb and he doesn't know how long he can hang on. The only thing really holding him up there are those little round rubber things on the sides of his goddamn sneakers! What are we gonna do?"

"C'mon, guys," said Larry. "We've got to think of something. Let's go up there. Find a rope or something. Anything. Anyone know where there's a rope?"

No one could think of any place to find a rope. Bingham suggested tying sheets together.

"Okay, you do that," Larry barked at him. "You guys," he said grabbing Downey and me, "we'll go up there and see what we can do. And, you guys," he said to Seth and Bradford, "stay right here and look like nothing's wrong. Try to keep anyone around here from looking up there."

I was glad Larry took charge and told us what to do. I certainly didn't have any ideas and would probably still be standing there with my mouth open, scratching my head, if he hadn't.

Seth ran off somewhere looking for sheets. Larry, Downey and I raced up to Bradford and Booger's room. The window was wide open and the room was freezing cold. Larry climbed halfway out the window and stayed there for a minute or so looking around. Back inside, he reported.

"Look, guys, there's got to be a way to get to him. Booger's left arm is only about three or four feet away and a little down from the window here, but there sure doesn't look like any way to get to him going sideways from here. It's too close to the edge. I think we've got to go up to the Nest and then get a rope or sheets or something down to him. It looks like he's maybe only five or six feet from the edge of the Nest and if we can get a rope to him, we could pull him up."

"We don't have a rope," I said.

"I know that, goddammit! But, we need a rope, or sheets, or something! Where is Bingham with the fucking sheets?"

. "Maybe Booger can't grab hold of anything, if his fingers are so numb," I said.

"Well, we've got to try, don't we? We just can't let him stay there and fall off, can we?"

"No, but how? Maybe someone's got to grab him so he doesn't have to use his hands," I said. "Maybe we could lower someone down there who could grab his wrists."

"Oh. Sure. You call up Charlton Heston and see if he's free to come over. Maybe he could make it sometime next week," said Larry acidly, remembering the hair-raising scenes in *The Greatest Show on Earth* we'd seen at the gym the night before. Charlton Heston had played the guy with steel nerves who catches people in a flying trapeze act. Maybe, I thought, the movie did have too much influence on me, but it did give me the idea.

"Hey, look," I said. "If his fingers are useless, how's he going to hang onto anything? How's he even going to catch a rope? Somebody's got to grab him so he doesn't have to move."

After a minute or two as we thought about it, Downey said, "Okay, I'll go down there since I'm sure you assholes are all too chicken to even consider it, but you guys better hold me by both legs and, for Christ's sake, don't let go. Okay?" No one argued.

Downey crawled up to the Eagle's Nest first, followed by Larry and me. He bent halfway over the ledge, put his forearms down on the slate roof and said, "Okay, let's go." Larry and I each picked up one of Downey's legs and began letting him inch headfirst on his elbows, wiggling very slowly down the roof toward Booger. All of a sudden, several chunks of slate tore off and clattered down onto Booger's arms and head. He didn't move a muscle or say anything.

"Don't worry, Booger," Downey whispered. "Don't move or look up or do anything. Just stay right there. When I get to you, I'm going to grab your arms and Larry and Bumppo are going to pull both of us back to the Nest together. You don't have to do anything but just hang on. Just hang on, Booger." Inch by inch, Downey kept talking to him, murmuring, "Just hang on, Booger…just hang on."

When he got close enough to make his move, he waved one hand at Larry and me to stop. Downey's head was now very close to Booger's. Downey's feet, which Larry and I were holding while bent over the edge of the Nest, were about three feet down the slope of the roof from the safe ledge of the Nest. I couldn't reach much farther. Even though it was freezing cold, I was sweating buckets from holding Downey's right foot and the fear that his pants would tear loose or that somehow I'd lose my grip. I had one hand around his ankle and the other on his low-cut boot. As Downey got ready to grab Booger's wrists, he raised his head and shoulders and the upper part of his body, lunged for both of Booger's wrists and gave an unexpected, sharp, involuntary kick with both his feet.

Larry yelled, "Whoa!" and swore, but he held on. I didn't.

Downey's kick had torn my right hand loose from his ankle and I grabbed at his boot with both hands. The boot came clean off in my hands with a force that sent me reeling, stumbling backwards until my back crashed into the brick chimney and I found myself sitting on the tar paper, looking with astonishment at the boot in my hands.

I closed my eyes, sure that in a second I would hear the terrible sound of Downey and Booger plunging down to the sidewalk about forty feet below. I sat frozen and senseless, and all of a sudden I was thinking of my brother! I saw Bob sliding slowly down those cold, gray slates looking up at me to save him. I was going to yell out loud to him that I'd save him. "Just hang on, Bob," I'd say. "I really will save you!" I meant to do something, but I didn't do anything. I couldn't. I just sat there frozen and watched as fog curled around Bob and he slipped over the edge, without a word, and disappeared into the gloom, staring at me with crazed, wild animal eyes full of hate.

"Shit, Bumppo—help! What the fuck are you doing?" Larry was shouting at me. He'd put one of his feet on the ledge of the Nest for leverage and had somehow horsed Downey up by one leg so that now he was close to the ledge, skewed awkwardly sideways. Downey's free leg and bare foot—his sock had come off with the boot—were thrashing the air; but, he still held on to Booger.

I snapped out of it, although for a few moments I wasn't sure what I was doing up there, it was so cold and dark, or even what was happening. Mechanically, I did what Larry told me and reached out and grabbed Downey's belt and hauled him up while Larry reached over Downey, grabbed Booger under the armpits and yanked him into the Nest with one tremendous heave.

Booger wasn't in any shape to go down the roof to his room for a long time, until he stopped shaking and he could feel and move his fingers that he warmed in his crotch. Even then, we were worried about his collapsing or slipping again and we all stayed close as we went down that time.

None of us ever went up to the Eagle's Nest again. My own reason—which I certainly didn't tell anybody—was that I was afraid I'd see Bob up there again and think about why I couldn't even try to save him. Larry had seen that something had gone wrong for me up there. Soon after, he asked me about it. I didn't want to tell him. How could he have understood it? I told him I didn't want to talk about it. "Why the hell not?" he asked, getting a little angry.

"Because it's none of your business," I answered.

"The hell it isn't! Whatever you were doing was really scary. I might not have been able to handle Booger alone. So, what the hell happened?"

I didn't say anything. After a long pause while he glowered at me, he said, "Okay, if that's the way you feel about it..." He never mentioned it again, but our relationship was never the same. There was always that unanswered question between us.

I did want to talk to somebody about what had happened to me up there. Maybe Dr. Heyl, though when I'd talked to him before —about Bob and Lang and the suicide pact—it didn't seem to do much good. He'd just sat and puffed on his pipe and listened. He'd asked me to make another appointment, but I hadn't done that.

MY ALGEBRA I TEACHER, Mr. Hulburd, a gentle old man whose antacid breath made my stomach queasy, worried about me a lot and tried to help me understand quadratic equations, but I just wasn't interested in Algebra. Not even my fear of his standing over me and smothering me with the smell of Milk of Magnesia was enough to make me do the work. I also had a series of migraine headaches, one after the other, and they came on almost always just before, or during, Mr. Hulburd's math class. I began to wonder if Mr. Hulburd's breath had something to do with causing those incredible headaches, as if his breath was poison, rather than God punishing me for getting mad at something or, maybe, for lust. Anyway, whatever was causing the headaches, they came and knocked me out sometimes twice a week. They sure didn't help me in Algebra; I flunked it eventually and would have to repeat it next year, but, thank God, not with Mr. Hulburd.

Although I didn't flunk French I, going to that class was a nightmare. My young French teacher, Mr. MacCombie, had a cresting wave of shiny orange hair that towered at least four inches over his forehead threatening to break at any minute and blind him. Worse, he insisted on exaggerating the enunciation of words like "tu" and "quoi" with his lips pursed and puckered like a kissing gourami (of which I had two pairs in my aquarium at home) and on drawing his amazing flexible lips back tight into a leering grin for each of the "-ir" verbs. I was embarrassed for him and in terror of having to recite in class. He would stand next to a student he wanted to recite and make him pucker and leer until the whole class would explode with laughter.

English I was different. The reading assignments my English teacher, William Bates, gave us were great and I began to enjoy his class, even if he wasn't as swashbuckling as his brother, Robert Bates, also an English teacher at Exeter, who was a mountain climber. He'd just returned from a tragic attempt to climb K-2 in Pakistan, the second highest mountain in the world, during which one of the members of the expedition died near the summit. He'd given us a slide-show lecture on it, with many pictures of the Himalayas, which were amazing, as was his story of how they fell, roped together, over a ridge and might all have been killed except that the last man was somehow able to anchor the rope.

For my Mr. Bates, we read *The Adventures of Huckleberry Finn*, *The Canterbury Tales*, some of Poe's and Hawthorne's short stories, *Animal Farm*, *The Grapes of Wrath* and other great books. I didn't speak up in class very often, since I didn't want to let on that I'd finished reading whatever we were discussing. I didn't know if Mr. Bates would like my doing that.

My favorite book that Mr. Bates assigned was *Mutiny on the Bounty*. I liked it so much, I went on to read the other Nordhoff and Hall books in the Bounty Trilogy, *Men Against the Sea* and *Pitcairn's Island*, and then other books Nordoff wrote alone—*The Derelict* and *The Pearl Lagoon*—and Hall's *The Lost Island*, all of which are terrific to read when it's zero degrees outside and the snow reaches your waist. Wandering around dreaming about berry-brown, bare-breasted *wahines* with lovely hula hands dancing for me by torchlight on a beach on Tahiti kept me from losing my marbles totally.

Somehow, even though I flunked Algebra and learned next to nothing in French except strange lip extensions, my mediocre work in Latin and Ancient History and my good work in English got me through my Prep year as far as Exeter was concerned.

What I really learned was more how to get along with other boys, solid citizens like Bradford, Seth and Larry Fraser, as well as outlaws like Downey. I also learned how to play bridge pretty well. Overall, I thought I was on the route Bob had laid out before me of getting Gentleman's C's—I regarded the F in Algebra as a temporary embarrassment that I would overcome—and trying to have a good time.

ONE EVENING AFTER dinner during the early part of the summer soon after I'd returned home from Exeter, when I was doing nothing except sitting in a stupor watching *I Love Lucy* or some other mindless TV show with Mom and Dad, a man I'd heard of but never met named Dr. Ferdinand Kertess, who lived with his wife and two sons in a big house near us in Ardsley-on-Hudson, called me on the telephone. Mom thought there was some mistake when she answered the phone and Dr. Kertess asked for me. She was really surprised when she heard me talking to him and saying that, sure, I guess it would be okay if I went over to his house and, sure, I guess I could leave in a few minutes. She couldn't imagine what he wanted with me, being all of fourteen then; it was very strange to her. With a look of dismay she waved her hand and said I could go if I wanted to. He's German; maybe that has something to do with it, she muttered.

Mrs. Kertess opened the front door for me and pointed me toward their living room. "Ferd iss in dare," she said. "He von't bite." I tried to smile. Dr. Kertess was alone in a large dark, wood-paneled living room, sitting in one of four huge overstuffed wing-backed chairs placed around a highly polished circular inlaid wood coffee table. He stood up, bowed slightly and shook hands formally with me—did he really click his heels?—and invited me to sit in one of the empty chairs. When I sank down between the enormous wings of the chair, I felt very small and lost in this foreign place with this foreign person I did not know.

I stared at the ceiling; the white plaster had been shaped into an elaborate interlocking design. I'd never seen a ceiling like that. Mom was right; this was very strange. What was I doing with this large, old, German man with a very high forehead and a halo of wispy white hair flying in all directions from the sides of his head, a little like Albert Einstein's? He must be over seventy, I thought, which was as old as I thought people ever got.

"Vat are you called? Na-tan-yel?" he asked.

"No, no one actually calls me 'Nathaniel.' It's either 'Nat' or some people call me 'Bumppo,'—after Natty Bumppo, who was the hero of James Fenimore Cooper's *The Pathfinder* and *The Deerslayer*," I answered.

"Zo, you read a lot?"

"Yes, I guess I do read a lot, although I've never actually read either *The Pathfinder* or anything else Cooper wrote. No, that's not right. I did read *The Last of the Mohicans* two years ago, but mainly I read stuff that has been assigned in my English class. But, yes, I do read other stuff, too."

"Like vhat?" he asked.

"Well, I had to read *Mutiny on the Bounty* for class and I got interested in the Bounty story, so I read the other books Nordhoff and Hall wrote about it. They weren't assigned. I just wanted to read them."

"I like dat. Dat's very good," he said. "You are a sophomore next year, just like Hans?"

"Yes. I haven't seen Hans in a long time. How's he doing?" I asked. His older son, Hans, had been in my class at Hackley.

"He's okay. He goes out a lot and I don't see him much. Maybe, I can learn something about vhat's going on vith him by talking vith you. Dat's one reason I called you up. I vant to know vhat your generation tinks about tings."

It soon became clear to me that Dr. Kertess wasn't at all strange. He was just amazingly curious. He was a chemist and a businessman—not a medical doctor. He liked talking about baseball, politics, the Big Bang, aliens, the Cold War, the H-bomb, history, flowers, gardening and butterflies, tennis, philosophy, psychology, Shakespeare, golf, astrology and very good food—among a million other things. He read constantly and always was in the middle of two or three books at the same time, everything from Plato to poetry to Mickey Spillane. He'd decided to learn Russian that summer so he could read Tolstoy and Turgenev. His library was full of old leather-bound works of Goethe, Kant and Nietzsche in his native German. Volumes of philosophers like Aristotle, Plato, Seneca, Thomas Aquinas, Descartes, John Stuart Mill and Sartre were dog-eared with thumbing. There was also a Bible and a copy of the Koran, nestled together at the end of a shelf next to Kahlil Gibran. He was curious about our neighbors—he didn't know any of them well and, apparently, wasn't invited to the constant weekend cocktail parties in Ardsley—and what work they did and whether I liked them. He asked about my friends and what we did and what we thought and, especially, what I had read and what I was reading now. Had I been to Europe or traveled in the US? No? I must go to Europe soon, he urged, and we planned what I should see. Did I have a girlfriend? Yes? What's her name? Joann Sutherland. Wonderful. What's she like—is she smart? Yes. What baseball team did I like? The Dodgers. How did I think Brooklyn would do this year? Gil Hodges was my hero? Why?

Tell me about everything, he'd say, and I nearly did that night. I came to believe that he really wanted to know, that he was interested in everything, including me, and seemed to want to know as much about everything as he possibly could. My age didn't matter to him, so his age stopped mattering to me and my instinctive fear of this particular adult went away that evening. I left believing that he was my friend—an older friend, for sure, but still my own friend with whom I could talk openly without thinking about the huge difference in our ages and experience. We also laughed a lot. Dr. Kertess liked to laugh.

As we talked that first time, I wondered if his interest in me was as a scientist studying a specimen—he was a chemist, after all. So, I thought, maybe I'm just a way for him to learn about the habits of the local adolescent fauna—how likely was it that this highly educated old man was actually interested in getting to know me? I must bore him silly. When he mentioned that he also talked with a girl named Jewelle—younger than I was and the sister of another guy in my class at Hackley—who also lived nearby, just as he talked with me, I wondered if he was collecting a pair of everything, something like Noah. I also wondered what this Jewelle was like, but he didn't tell me. He kept things between them private. I liked that.

I went to see him again about two weeks later. When I got there Mrs. Kertess was in the kitchen cleaning up glasses and dishes. I asked her to let me help her and as I was wiping a glass, she asked me if Dr. Kertess had told me what had happened to him—really to them—during the War? I said he hadn't told me anything about it. She said I ought to know and began. It happened on a hot Saturday afternoon in the summer of 1942. They were outside their house in Ardsley and Dr. Kertess was reading in the garden. Two men in brown suits and hats driving a brown four-door sedan—she remembered that everything was brown—rang the bell at their front door. She'd gone to the door and the men asked for Dr. Kertess. She left them waiting outside and went back through the house to the garden and told Dr. Kertess that he had two visitors, but didn't know what they wanted. She remembered telling him that they were wearing suits and hats on that hot afternoon. Dr. Kertess went to see what they wanted. It was maybe ten or fifteen minutes later—she didn't remember how long—that she began to wonder what he was doing with the two men and perhaps another few minutes before she went to the front of the house to see. There was no sign of Dr. Kertess or the two men or the brown car. They were gone.

She didn't see him or speak to him for over three years, until months after the War ended in 1945. All she was told—and the first time she'd been told anything was months after he'd disappeared—was that he'd been taken into custody by U.S. Marshals as an enemy alien because he worked for a German chemical company and was interned along with other Germans who were considered security risks. She wasn't told for months where he was or even that he was alive and well. Later, she said she'd learned that he had spent most of that time in a maximum security section of the federal prison at Ft. Leavenworth, Kansas. He'd spent almost four years there. She told me that he'd never been accused of any crime or given a trial and wasn't allowed to speak to anyone but prison officials—three years without being allowed any contact with his wife and children. When he was released, he'd lost a lot of his black hair and what remained had turned thin and pure white. He'd aged by many years, she said. When I met him, I thought he was well over seventy, but he was actually just fifty-four years old. He told her that being cut off from his family, books, newspapers, the radio, music and virtually all human contact—from life itself—was so horrible that he couldn't bear to think or talk about it. He'd told her the facts, about how he'd lived and almost gone insane, and then asked her not to speak about it ever again. He'd vowed, she said, to live and enjoy life as fully as he possibly could and she said he treated every day as if two men in brown suits were going to pick him up and put him away somewhere forever. She said he'd told his sons not to expect anything when he died—if there was any money left, he'd made a mistake.

That night, I told Dr. Kertess about the Eagle's Nest and what had happened there. He seemed most interested in the part about Bob and my "seeing" him go over the edge of the roof as I sat there stupidly doing nothing.

"Vhat's that all about?" he asked seriously. "Vhy should you feel guilty about your brother? He's, vhat, four, fife years older than you are? Vhat's to feel guilty about? And, iss he dying?"

"No, of course, not. He's not really dying. I just think he's had a tough time at home and he doesn't know what he wants to do. I mean he doesn't seem to want to do anything, so it's not like he doesn't know if he wants to be a lawyer or a doctor or a banker or whatever. He says he knows for sure that he doesn't want to be or do anything he can think of. That's different."

"He'll get over it. Ve all haff doubts at hiss age. But, vhat about you? Vhy do you feel like he's going over the edge, and you could save him if you try?"

"It doesn't sound right, when you say it like that. I hope he's not really going over the edge and, if he was, I don't know what I could do to save him. Sure, I'd want to help him, but what could I actually do?"

"I tink your dream or vhatever it vas iss telling you dat you are very vorried about him and vhat direction he's going in and you can do noting to help him. So you must sit and vatch him go over de edge. In your dream, you haff no other choice. But, Bumppo, you know you always haff other choices, and so does he."

While I sat surrounded by the enormous wing chair feeling very small, Dr. Kertess got out of his chair and walked around behind it. Leaning on the back of the chair, he looked at me.

"Maybe, dere's something else. Maybe, you are afraid of what might happen to you if you follow your brother wherever he's going. Maybe, you don't vant to follow him 'over de edge.' You should tink about it."

I LEFT FOR Camp Keewaydin, a canoe camp in Ontario way north of Toronto on huge Lake Temagami, in mid-June. I went with Bert Hand, Hans Kertess and several other boys from Ardsley. It was a summer that I still think about sometimes, even after more than half a century. I remember the great fishing for bass, walleyes and, sometimes, northern pike on lakes we were sure had been seen only by Indians before us. Our counselor, Fred Bowden, who was a recent graduate of a college in Maine, got our respect by showing us that he either knew what to do in any situation or could figure it out. Our section had seven canoes— twelve boys, Fred and a Ojibway Indian guide named Joe who was in his sixties, didn't like to work a lot, spoke very little and had no use for us. I was Joe's bowman, which meant that I did a lot of work pulling him along as he sat back and steered. On portages, I carried the pots, pans and dishes, which were Joe's responsibility, in a big wooden box, called a "wannigan," on my back with a leather strap, called a "tumpline," around my forehead distributing the weight of the wannigan to my neck and shoulders. We rarely stayed in the same place for two nights in a row. If we didn't find an existing campsite to use, we made our own. In either case, we always left our campsites neat and clean, chiefly because of Fred's rule that we leave each place better than we found it. He had another rule I remember, which was to do everything as well as we could. That applied mainly to making privies, which Fred called "forts," building stone fire pits for cooking, setting up our tents and the other tasks of camping, but both his rules have stayed with me ever since.

I had a sense of physical danger that whole summer. One of the first things we were taught was how to be safe in a canoe, how to paddle it, sit in it, right it if it swamps, carry it and repair it. We were also told what not to do, such as diving for things that fall into the water.

We'd heard that one of the older boys who was on the all-summer trip to Hudson Bay had died in a terrible accident, but how he died wasn't part of the story. Whenever I looked down through the water and could see fields of tall green grass waving in the currents below, I would speculate that maybe it was the eel grass that got him; it could wind itself around a thrashing ankle and hold a person fast. At midsummer, we heard that the boy dove into a river to retrieve a wannigan that sank when a canoe tipped over. The river looked placid enough, apparently, but when he got under water, on the way down to the wannigan, a swift current caught him and swept him into an underwater niche hollowed out of the sheer rock of the riverbank and he couldn't get out.

That story stayed with me for the rest of the summer and made me, and my pals, very careful, at least most of the time. I forgot myself once when I went fishing alone at dusk one evening. I paddled a canoe around the back of an island and began to fish in the clear, still water between the island and the shore. I could see my red and white "Daredevil" lure jiggling along as I retrieved it along the edge of a weed bed. Two or three times, I'd cast and reel the lure in, watching it pass the weeds twitching it now and then. Suddenly, a torpedo shot out from the weeds and I saw the white of the lure careening out of the shallows toward the open water of the lake. I pulled back and set the hook, feeling the weight of the fish for the first time. I was so exited, I stood up in the canoe—one of the dumbest things I could have done. But, I was lucky and stumbled or tripped on a thwart and found myself on my knees in the middle of the canoe, which was being towed away from shore, clutching my rod to my chest. For a moment, I thought of cutting the line and paddling back to safety, but that passed soon enough. I held the rod with my left hand with my thumb on the reel trying to slow the fish down while I grabbed the paddle with my right hand and did my best to halt its progress out into the lake. It worked and, slowly, I was able to play the fish and still maneuver the canoe in a path toward the shore. When I got a few feet from shore, again I didn't know what to do. How could I get out of the canoe onto the shore while the fish was still fighting? So, I got as close to shore as I could and swamped the canoe—tipped it over and spilled out holding my rod with both hands. I felt for the bottom and found that I could barely stand; the water was up to my armpits. I held the rod with both arms over my head and waded as best I could toward shore. When the water was only knee deep, I stopped wading and brought the fish in. It was the largest northern pike I'd ever seen and looked like a huge evil monster. I worried that it might try to take a chunk out of my calf with its wickedly sharp teeth. But, seeing that it was tired of fighting and not apparently about to bite me, I reached down and grabbed the lure to try to unhook the fish and release it. The fish flinched and thrashed and the lure promptly flew out of its mouth and embedded itself in the heel of my hand. I watched as the noble creature treaded water for a few moments and then, with one swish of its powerful tail, disappeared, leaving me to swim about a hundred yards out into the lake in the darkening gloom to retrieve the empty canoe. It's become a mystical memory over the years, a moment of tremendous excitement and satisfaction, knowing that I coped with unfamiliar and potentially serious problems successfully.

I came home from camp stronger and tanner than I'd left. I also felt that I probably could handle anything that came my way; if it was something I didn't know about, I felt sure I could figure it out.

Chapter Four

WHEN I GOT back to Exeter that fall, I had to repeat Algebra—no surprise there—but, thank God, not with Mr. Hulburd. However, even with a new teacher who was fairly normal, I still got nauseous from quadratic equations that in my mind smelled of Milk of Magnesia. I was also in the idiot section of French II, which was fine because all my friends were there, too, and I would be taking Latin II and European History. Larry Fraser was going to be my roommate and our double room was in Webster Hall, right next to Dunbar where I'd spent the last year.

Apart from playing bridge, my real love was English II. Chilson Leonard was my teacher. The first time I saw him, he looked huge and rugged. His tweed jacket didn't quite fit and there was a book crammed into the jacket pocket. He looked like he'd have been more comfortable in a mackinaw with an ax in his hand. But, in spite of his daunting looks, and his usual scowl which did nothing to make him more approachable, I found myself wanting to please him, wanting to do my best. In fact, I wanted to be reading something all the time. To continue reading, I sometimes just didn't go to other classes, although you really weren't supposed to "cut" any classes at Exeter.

I did the most unbelievable things to be able to read. I would sneak out of my room at night and go the library—the library!—where I'd have to hide in a nook so I wouldn't get caught. I found an old red leather chair with a floor lamp in an alcove surrounded on three sides by floor-to-ceiling books no one ever looked at. I'd curl up there for hours and forget the time and whatever I was actually supposed to be doing. Sometimes, I'd even beg off my regular bridge game on which I had come to depend for comradeship and a small but fairly steady income. I cut sports, a sin that, if discovered, resulted in getting a notice of delinquency, manually signed with a flourish by the Athletic Director himself, one Nicholas P. Moutis. Like everyone else, I pretended to treat his "Moutis Noutices" with contempt, but I was actually somewhat leery of them since six was the limit per term.

My absolutely favorite thing to do that second year at Exeter—my sophomore year, called the "Lower Middle" year—and I did it a lot, was to jump on my bed alone in my room when Larry Fraser was playing football or basketball and read with my old Webcor phonograph blasting out something that seemed appropriate to what I was reading. Doris Day's "Secret Love" went well with *Romeo and Juliet.* The best was reading *Lorna Doone,* full of the incredibly wild and dark English moors of the seventeenth century with a cast of bloodthirsty outlaws terrorizing Bagworthy Forest, while playing my 45-RPM record of Waldyr

Azevedo's (I loved that name) song "Delicado" over and over until the record wore out. Although the connection between the insistent Spanish beat of that song and the savagery and intrigue of Blackmore's nineteenth century romantic novel was completely lost on Larry, I can tell you that it was there for me. "Delicado" somehow transported me back three hundred years to savage and bloody Exmoor, away from bleak and bloodless Exeter, New Hampshire, and the impending catastrophe that any fool but me would have seen coming. Sometimes, I'd eat Lorna Doone cookies when I was reading the book, but I never did find out any connection between the book and the cookies.

When I wasn't reading, I was usually playing bridge. Many of my bridge games, which were not supposed to be for money since gambling of any sort was against the rules, took place in the basement buttrooms (out-of-bounds for me) of various dorms, including Wentworth Hall, which was Mr. Leonard's dormitory. At the beginning of that year, Mr. Leonard would scowl when he saw me coming or going to Wentworth or somewhere else on the campus, and I seemed to bump into him a lot. Maybe, I looked guilty of something and he picked up on that or, maybe, he thought I should be in my room studying more. I felt guilty about playing bridge so much and was sure that Mr. Leonard would see me hanging around with my bridge buddies, all of whom were a class ahead of me, and figure it out. Whatever he suspected, however, I felt that he thought that I couldn't possibly be doing much homework for his class or anyone else's. I could see suspicions cloud his eyes when he looked at me—the same change that happened to Dad's eyes when he suspected, but wasn't sure, that I'd done something wrong. Mr. Leonard didn't know the half of it. He didn't even have a glimmer about the un-told hours I sat watching Larry eat three peanut-betweens and three burgers at the same time at the Grill, or the hours I curled up in the library or the hours I hung around with my pals, let alone the chunks of time I spent playing bridge.

Mr. Leonard was right, of course, that I went a little too easy on my work for other teachers, but, for him, I did all my work, and much more, and did it well, and I think he came to know it. While I didn't like to talk in class much, I was always ready to answer his questions, and he asked a lot of them. It was his way of teaching, and it was hard to hide from him since we all sat around a big oval wooden table. He would ask us why some char-acter did something or why the author chose to kill off a char-acter and what we thought it all meant. He almost never came right out and told us anything, and we left many classes wonder-ing about the answers and whether we'd gotten them right. As I was reading, I got used to imagining the kinds of questions he'd ask in class, so I'd be ready to answer when he called on me. It usually worked.

As the year went on and the fall turned colder and winter be-gan, I noticed that sometimes he'd go out of his way to talk to me in the Grill or other places where I'd bump into him. He'd look at me with his sad, sagging bloodhound eyes and ask me some joshing question about whatever we were reading in his class, but sometimes I had a feeling that he wasn't just kidding around. It was like he was probing, looking for something. At first, I'm sure he was trying to catch me in some clever trap and unmask me as the charlatan he believed deep down I was. But, as time went on, I began to feel more comfortable with him and believed that he truly enjoyed bantering with me, although he still seemed a little suspicious of me. Sometimes, I played into his suspicions, mostly because I thought he knew I liked him and that he enjoyed it. I didn't think he was as tough and mean as hell as everyone said he was. He was supposed to be a real grouch, in fact, which is why almost everyone except me avoided him as much as possible outside class. When I could handle his questions—he especially loved to ask me about minor characters who'd been mentioned only once or twice in a long book—he seemed to like that a lot. Best of all, when I could answer a question he thought pretty difficult, I'd see a sparkle in his eyes peering out at me from the wrinkles on his face. That was wonderful. It was like a small victory for me and I knew he was pleased. At those times, I'd think that, maybe, he wasn't trying to trap me after all, but was playing some kind of mental game with me, a secret game he enjoyed playing as much as I did. I felt there was something special between us, that I was the kind of student that made teachers like him keep teaching. That was a good feeling.

Mr. Leonard liked poetry a lot. That surprised me. Here was this really big, tough and mean guy with huge rough hands who wore a red and black plaid mackinaw and a fur hat in the winter and looked like a lumberjack, but who carried around a book wherever he went, and it was usually poetry, which I thought was for fags until Mr. Leonard made us read some. He could talk for hours about a single poem, drawing amazing information and meaning from just a few words. He really opened my eyes, and I began to read some poetry myself.

Most of my bridge bunch had to be inventive to get by without doing much. A few had perfected the art of appearing to be downright grinds while doing almost nothing—an art that I appreciated but never learned properly. They always talked to teachers and asked about their wives and kids. They went to the teas faculty wives gave and they joined clubs, like the Literary Society and the French Club. The faculty loved these guys. A lot of teachers were completely hoodwinked and thought that playing bridge was a natural and appropriate avocation for these budding intellectual members of the ruling class. So, while they spent at least as much time as I did at the card table, they were accepted as quiet, scholarly and solidly legitimate members of the Exeter elite and their grades were excellent.

For those like me, who didn't do all that brownnosing, our grades were not so good and we were generally regarded as budding outlaws. I can't tell you how annoying it was when those other guys got comments on their papers from teachers such as "highly perceptive," "inspired," "fresh" and "unique insight." One of them was encouraged to "explore" his "brilliant speculative powers." The truth, of course—and even they knew it—was that their work was sheer, utter nonsense, and, except for what they could glean from a trot, born of almost total ignorance. Whatever they said or wrote came out of left field, and thus was bound to be "unique" and "speculative." I couldn't help wondering if, maybe, the teachers got bored reading the papers and examinations of students who knew what they were talking about.

If it was possible to get good grades and the teachers' respect without working, that sounded fine to me. The brownnosers certainly did have an undeniable brilliance (which, of course, I felt I did, too) since it wasn't easy to hoodwink most of the faculty consistently without slipping up sometimes and being exposed.

They lived precariously and that appealed to me, as did the notion that I was in on the joke, an insider bound by a secrecy as sacred as the law of *omerta* for the members of the real Mob. Truly, I thought, those guys had solved the puzzle of actually enjoying life at Exeter, and I became an eager apprentice. But, I wanted to do it without all the brownnosing. That was a big mistake. That was an essential ingredient; as it turned out, so was studying. No one told me that.

One of the most successful of my bridge bunch was a New York City kid who had gone to Buckley and who played bridge with an intensity I've never seen equaled. He had dedicated himself to learning everything about the game, and read every book and newspaper column he could find about it. He knew even the most arcane bidding conventions and never resorted to using any illegal signals or bids with any member of our fraternity —only against outsiders. He also harbored an equally intense passion for art, but he kept that well hidden from all of us. If we'd only known that he went to faculty teas because he liked them or known that he was sneaking off surreptitiously to study paintings, while the rest of us sought out the most lurid pornography we could find, he would have been summarily exiled from the group. I knew I'd never tell any of them how much time I spent in my nook at the library and wondered if some of the other guys were also sneaking off doing something like that and not telling us.

The most dangerous member of my mob was "Black Sam" Saxon, also a New York City kid, who demonstrated his particular brilliance simply by not getting arrested for some serious crime, let alone merely avoiding expulsion before graduation.

Sam was only two years older than I, but he was big and strong and had an extraordinary amount of wiry black hair all over his body, particularly his back. He had an extremely heavy beard and always looked as if he needed a shave. Of course, he looked about ten years older than anyone else, and this helped him pursue his various appetites in places I was not usually allowed to enter because of my age, unless I were to use my phony driver's license, which I hadn't tried to do yet.

Sam had enormous, voracious, insatiable appetites—for alcohol, tobacco, women, cars, and, in fact, everything that was absolutely illegal at Exeter—but not for virtually anything Exeter thought worthy or even allowed. He hated being at Exeter, and everything about it. He hated teachers because they were teachers, obviously incompetent to do anything better than to retreat utterly from real life to this grimly dull New England hamlet and persecute children. He hated the process of learning, which was either much too slow for him or totally useless in the real world and a waste of his time. Having to go to school anywhere kept him from gulping down the whole world in one bite and getting to the point of it all—making money, lots of money; the rest was just beside the point.

Sam led a bunch of us to the Rough Rider Room at the Roosevelt Hotel next to Grand Central Station after the long train ride back to New York at the beginning of the Thanksgiving break that year. Bradford, Larry and I, with about ten other kids from Exeter who lived in or near New York, were all crammed around a bunch of little round cocktail tables in the middle of that busy cocktail lounge at about five o'clock in the afternoon. A pretty but harassed waitress in a short skirt and net stockings said "Hello,

Sam," with a suggestive lilt. He ordered a bottle of Scotch for himself and drinks for the rest of us; I'd asked for a whiskey sour. He had to bully the waitresses a bit into serving us because none of us even looked close to legal age. Black Sam not only knew the waitress there but had also "dated" her, a date he decided to tell us all about. It was the first and would be the last time I went to the Rough Rider Room.

After the waitress left to get our drinks, Black Sam started quietly telling us about her. He said he'd taken her home to Brooklyn in a cab after the lounge closed, walked her up the stairs to her brownstone apartment and gone inside with her. Slowly, Sam's voice rose and his eyes began to take on a shiny, crazed look as he really got wound up and began telling us how he'd taken her clothes off and described the lady's spectacular naked body.

The lady herself had returned to our table with a tray loaded with drinks. She stood not five feet from us, paralyzed with disbelief and humiliation at what she was hearing. Sam's voice was now rising above the din of cocktail lounge, packed with tired, harried commuters grabbing a quick drink before having to dash for their trains. He used his hands theatrically, delicately, to describe the delights of her torso in minute, erotic detail. Even some men at nearby tables strained to listen. Sam moved from her "rosy-peaked, lust-swollen breasts" down her ribcage "heaving with hot anticipation," to her "perfect navel and the beginning of a precious little trail of golden fleece which trickled down to her..." Sam never finished. Instead, he stood up, his eyes blazing and locked on that poor, transfixed woman.

For a moment, I couldn't tell what in the world he was going to do. It looked like he was thinking about picking her up and plunking her down in the middle of our table to show us what he was talking about when words failed him. Or, more likely I thought, he had whipped himself up into such a frenzy that he'd completely forgotten us or where he was and was going to try to do again, right there, whatever he had done with her that night in Brooklyn.

I was mesmerized and heard myself think, "Wow, this is great!" At that moment, I looked at the waitress and my eyes froze. She was standing so close I could have touched her. Her shoulders were slightly stooped, and wisps of brown hair were wet with the perspiration on her forehead. Her bra strap had fallen down her arm from the sleeve of her frayed little black, short-skirted waitress' outfit and she'd smudged her lipstick somehow. She was staring at Sam, confused, with her mouth open. Whatever she was thinking, I could tell that she was struggling, trying somehow to blot out the painful reality of what she was seeing and hearing. Then, as her mind no longer allowed her to doubt what was happening, she stooped further and her face became the saddest, loneliest face I'd ever seen. She was so alone.

I wanted to put my arms around her and tell her that it was all in fun. No one meant to hurt her. Sam was crazy sometimes, but everything would be alright, I'd see to that. I'd stay with her and she wouldn't be so alone or sad. I wanted to do that, but I couldn't. It was as if I wasn't really there.

A moment after Black Sam stood up, a three-piece suited gentleman, who was sitting nearby with his hat, coat and briefcase in his lap probably having a drink while he was waiting for a train to Hastings or Dobbs Ferry, apparently decided, rightly, that whatever Sam had on his mind was big trouble for the wait-ress and that her insulted femininity needed defending. The man swung his briefcase at Sam and hit him a glancing blow on the shoulder and side of his head. Sam flinched, curled his lip in rage, and pounced on the man, growling and knocking him out of his chair and onto the floor, upsetting a table and dozens of glasses, some quite full, which went flying in all directions. Other tables were upset and other drinks started spilling as people got up and moved too quickly trying to avoid getting wet, or just to get out of there. It was like a fight scene in an old Western: Chairs were being overturned, women were screaming, everyone was trying to get out through one small door all at the same time. It was great!

It was also horrible—not so much because I was afraid I'd get hurt, but because of what I saw in the eyes of Larry, Bradford and some of the other Exeter guys who were there. In an eerie way, I disconnected from what was happening and retreated to some safe, isolated place where it was quiet and I was watching Sam humiliate her and the chaos that followed as if I were watch-ing a movie, but one that made my heart ache. From this remote place, I could see the wild, hard, glassy eyes of my best friends, smiling, full of excitement and lust as Sam described her body. Later, I watched Bradford take a few cheap, furtive punches at the bodies swirling around him and he grinned at me when they connected. Larry put his huge leg out, hoping to trip somebody. Another Exeter guy, grinning madly, poured a drink in a man's jacket pocket as he was getting up off the floor. How could they do that? And they loved doing it! They just didn't seem to care that they might be hurting someone. They didn't seem to feel the

pain Sam inflicted on that poor, miserable waitress or to understand any connection between their hard, sneaky punches and
the real pain they caused. I saw in a flash that, given the right
circumstances, my friends, most of them not rich or warped or
anything, but kids just like me—my own best friends—could
become a lynch mob, doing horrible things to other human be-
ings. Was I like that, too? I wanted to stand up and say, in a very
sensible and reasonable, yet authoritative, tone of voice, "Say,
Sam, I think it would be a real good idea for you to stop pum-
meling that poor guy and apologize to this pretty waitress here."
I knew no one would hear me or, if they did, they'd think I'd lost
my mind and ignore me anyway. No, there was really nothing I
could do.

Nothing bad ever happened to Sam because of that incident,
and it became part of the folklore of Exeter as it grew and
changed in the retelling and was transformed into another minor legend. Sam marked it down in his own annals as at least
comparable to the scene his own father had caused when he had
brought three prostitutes and a carload of bootleg liquor from
Boston back to Exeter in an open-topped yellow Stutz Bearcat
when he had been a student there during Prohibition. A riot had
broken out when Sam's father stood up in the rumble seat of the
Stutz and began to auction off the girls and the booze.

Sam, of course, was a menace to all right-thinking people and
an orderly society. That he survived to graduate from Exeter
still seems an impossible accomplishment due, I truly believe,
only to his genius for doing things that were so extravagant and
so outrageous that no one could believe them. At any rate, Sam
was a great bridge player and I found myself drawn to him for

some reason I didn't understand. Chilson Leonard had seen me with Sam many times; he probably thought Sam was one of my best pals.

MR. LEONARD LOVED Robert Frost's poems and, probably, could talk for hours about any of them. One day in class he read "Nothing Gold Can Stay." I was stunned by Frost's observation that the first things that grow in the spring aren't green, they are yellow: "Nature's first green is gold." I thought about that line and realized that was something only a poet could say— not a painter, composer, novelist or botanist. It gave me my first feeling that poetry could be rewarding. Another day, he read "Stopping by Woods on a Snowy Evening." His gruff bass voice created a vivid mental picture of the solitary man pausing for a moment in the silent calm of woods on a dark, snowy night. Leonard's wrinkled face and heavy eyelids made him look sad— maybe, a little depressed—matching the melancholy mood of the poem. I could see Mr. Leonard himself standing in those woods and could hear the "easy wind" in his voice. He seemed to belong to woods and loneliness. And, there was something dark about him also, something that hinted at some battle he still had to fight with himself, maybe depression or loneliness. When he came to the lines at the end, it was as if Mr. Leonard was speaking his own mind, telling us that he was weary of life. Although death—which, I thought, was symbolized by the "lovely, dark and deep" woods—was pulling at him, he would still go on; he had "miles to go and promises to keep" before he could sleep forever. When he was finished and we started talking about the rhyme scheme and Frost's use of alliteration, I found it hard to listen. I thought I had just glimpsed something of his soul.

I began to read some poetry on my own, to my great surprise. I read Keats' "Ode on a Grecian Urn," which was in our book, but Mr. Leonard hadn't assigned to us. It confused me. I understood that Keats was intrigued with the little figures painted on the ancient Greek vase, frozen in time—"for ever warm…and for ever young…" But, the end baffled me. What could he have meant by the lines at the end that go: "Beauty is truth, truth beauty—that is all / Ye know on earth and all ye need to know"? It sounded good, and really profound, but the more I thought about it, the more I thought either it was just not right or, more likely, I just didn't get it. There's got to be more than truth and beauty, I thought. Something's got to be bigger and more important. What about God? So, pretty sure that I didn't really understand the poem, I asked Mr. Leonard about it one day after class. At first, I'm sure he thought I was trying to brownnose him by asking about a poem he hadn't assigned to us yet. He seemed fidgety, like he wanted to pack his bookbag and get out of the classroom and get on to wherever he was going. When he saw that I really wanted to know what it meant, he perked up a bit. So, he let me babble on about how could Keats really have thought that truth was beauty and vice versa and that's all we need on earth. Leonard put down his green bookbag and sat down again in his chair and smiled. He looked like he was actually warming up a bit, which was pretty unusual for him. He pointed to the bookshelf in the corner and told me to go get a volume of Archibald MacLeish's poetry for him, which I did. He thumbed through it until he came to what he was looking for, bent the book back double at the page and handed it to me. It was "Ars Poetica," a short poem about what a poem is. It says: "A poem should be wordless / like the flight of birds" which wasn't too helpful since it was pretty hard for me to understand how a poem could be "wordless." After I'd read it, Mr. Leonard looked at me and recited the last line from memory: "A poem should not mean, but be." He asked me what I thought about that.

I did think about it for a minute. "I guess it means that I shouldn't be asking what Keats meant, but asking myself what it means to me. But, that didn't make a lot of sense either. I can't seem to get past thinking that Keats was saying something that just isn't right."

"Do you listen to music," he asked?

"Sure," I said, and I told him about the connections I'd made between *Lorna Doone* and the music of "Delicado" and between *The Scarlet Letter*, the book we'd just started reading in his class then, and both "Cara Mia" and "Sh-Boom," depending on what was going on between Hester and Mr. Dimmesdale. He winced a bit, but smiled.

"No," he said, "I mean good music, chamber music, symphonies—Bach, Beethoven and Brahms?"

"Well," I said, "I've heard some of that kind of music in church, and my mother sometimes plays serious things on the piano, but I don't listen to it voluntarily."

"You should try it and ask yourself what it means."

"What do you mean, 'what it means'? How can music mean something?"

"What about paintings—have you been through the art gallery here yet," he asked.

I was on sure ground. "Yes, sir, I go there a lot. Mrs. Baker's a friend of my father's." Mrs. Baker was the widow of one of Dad's classmates at Harvard; when he died in a plane crash, Dad had recommended her for the job of starting up and running a small art gallery at Exeter. She had been nice to me when I first arrived and had asked me for tea several times, which was a little trying, but I went because I liked her.

"What about the art on the walls—do you look at the paintings?"

"Yes, she's got a bunch of paintings of New Hampshire, some by teachers here. I've looked at all of them."

"Well," he said, "do they have any meaning for you?"

Now I was lost again. "I just don't understand what you mean when you ask me what music or a painting 'means.' They don't 'mean' anything—they just are; they exist and don't mean anything. But, they're different. A poem is supposed to 'mean' something. Isn't that right?"

He leaned back and folded his big, rough hands. He looked at his fingers twitching for a long minute and then, looking pretty serious.

"Music and art convey meaning in their own ways," he said. "They are different forms of communication, different languages. Perhaps, they enter your brain through different senses, but they do communicate, just as literature communicates, and the best communicate truth. Truth about the world we live in, truth about life, truth about God. The best art of all kinds conveys an aesthetic experience—'a vision of truth flashed on the inner eye,' someone once said. So, it's not scientific truth but emotional truth—a 'vision of truth' experienced emotionally—that only art can convey. I think that's what Keats meant, and it's also close to what MacLeish meant that a poem should 'be.' It either gives you 'a vision of truth flashed on the inner eye,' or it doesn't. If it does, that's what Keats says is the essence of beauty, which can only exist if there is truth. He found that beauty/truth on ancient Greek pottery; many people find it in the works of Bach or the paintings of Monet. Understand now?"

I said I'd think about what he'd said and maybe we could talk about it again when I'd thought more about it. He said that would be fine—anytime.

"In fact," he said, "why not come see me at home next week. We'll talk some more. How about four o'clock next Tuesday?"

When the afternoon of that day came, I left the Grill where I'd watched Larry wolf three peanut-betweens and went to see Mr. Leonard. I'd re-read Keats' poem a few times and was thinking about it, but getting no "vision of truth flashed" on my "inner eye." When I'd reached Mr. Leonard's door I was about to knock when I heard voices—or rather, Mr. Leonard's voice. It was low and menacing and sounded like a growl. I couldn't hear what he was saying, but I could tell that Mr. Leonard wasn't at all happy with whoever was on the other end of the phone line. I thought maybe I should leave and turned to go. A little girl, about seven or eight, with blonde hair in pigtails was standing next to me. "Hi," I said, a bit startled. She didn't say anything for a moment and then looked up at me and asked: "How come you're here?"

"To see Mr. Leonard. He's my English teacher."

"Why? No one ever comes to see him."

"Why not?" I asked.

"I dunno. Maybe because he gets mad when people come here."

"Why should he get mad when someone comes to see him?" I hoped no one in the house could hear my nosy question.

"I dunno. I'm not supposed to talk about it."

"Talk about what?"

She was looking at her feet and didn't say anything. Then she looked up and her eyes went past me. She'd seen something over my shoulder. She shuddered and ran away across the lawn toward her house. I turned around and saw Mr. Leonard looking at me through a crack in the doorway. I couldn't see his face clearly.

"Hi, Mr. Leonard," I said. "I was just having a chat with your little neighbor. Do you want me to come back some other time?"

"Why the hell are you here?" he almost snarled, opening the door and standing in the middle of the doorway, blocking it. Behind him, I could see a chair with lots of papers stacked by it.

"Today's when you said I should come over to talk some more about Keats," I said, trying to sound upbeat with weak knees.

He didn't answer and stood in the doorway stroking his hands, one against the other, time after time. He looked like he was off somewhere thinking about something, but from the glower on his face and the hardness of his eyes, I didn't think it was poetry. He looked like he wanted to break something.

"Maybe I should come back later. You've probably got a lot of other things you want to do?" I suggested tentatively.

After a long moment he said in a softer voice, "That's right. It would be a good idea if you came back later. Sorry, but I have to do something." So, I left.

I didn't know who or what was bothering him, but it seemed

to involve other people, maybe his wife or kids. Did he have kids? I didn't know. I'd never seen any kids of his playing around Webster with the other faculty brats. I felt like the little girl, frightened when I saw Mr. Leonard in the doorway. I also sensed the bitter fog of repressed anger and hate lurking inside Mr. Leonard's apartment—it reeked of it. I knew that fog. I'd grown up with it, but I didn't know that other people had it too.

After that encounter, I noticed that Mr. Leonard didn't seem to be suspicious of me any more. It was as if my asking about Keats and actually going to see him made me closer to him. He took me aside after class soon after I'd gone to his house and apologized for not asking me in and having our talk about Keats. I told him I was sorry to have come at a bad time.

"Have you been thinking some about Keats and our last discussion?"

"Yes, sir," I said. "I've been trying to understand what you said and trying to see if I can get a 'vision of truth' on my 'inner eye,' but I haven't had much luck with that." He seemed amused by my effort. His face wrinkled up so much I could hardly see his eyes.

Mr. Leonard started calling on me more in class. He seemed to take me more seriously, as if my opinions mattered. I read more and more, reading as much for him as myself, eager to be called on because I knew I was really on top of whatever we were doing. And, my grades showed it, at least in English.

He assigned papers for us to write at least every week and, unlike Mr. Bates and, I think, all the other English teachers who used letter grades, Mr. Leonard graded us with numbers. My grades, which had been mostly in the 80's, crept into the low 90's. No one was doing better. I was neck and neck with the kid who got the best marks in our class, a greasy grind, of course. In late December, just before Christmas vacation, Mr. Leonard announced our grades for the term. My average for the term was 87. The grind's average was 86. Bradford grabbed me as we were walking out of the classroom that day, held my right arm up and shouted, "THE WINNAH AND CHAM...PEEN!"

Then things changed.

Chapter Five

ONE COLD, CLEAR January afternoon, when I was walking with Larry back to our room from the Grill where I'd watched him eat a little snack of four peanut-betweens and three large Cokes, we saw Mr. Leonard in his red and black plaid mackinaw, swinging his green bookbag like a woodsman's axe, ambling loosely along another concrete path that led toward Webster Hall. He waved to us.

When I saw him, I stopped. Larry kept going, hoping to avoid Mr. Leonard. I said hello back to him, getting ready for some tricky question about something in the last pages of *Moby-Dick* to see if I'd read that far. Instead of bantering, he was straightforward and asked me how I was coming along with *Moby-Dick*. "Ready for the quiz tomorrow?" he asked.

Sure that he would relish a little banter, I looked at him aghast and said,"*Moby-Dick*? Quiz tomorrow? Holy Cow. At least I've got a couple of hours to read it tonight...Oh no! It's bridge night!"

I was expecting a smile that would tell me he knew I was joshing him as I usually did. But, there was no smile. He looked disgusted. But, no bomb went off and he didn't attack me or start frothing at the mouth. He didn't laugh either, but his eyes changed. The open and curious look I'd grown to recognize as almost, but not quite, warm was gone in an instant. Now his eyes were flat. I couldn't see behind them. He shrugged his shoulders, frowned and nodded his head a little and continued walking on toward Wentworth Hall. As I watched him walk away, I could feel him go back to doubting me. I had a tremendous urge to call out: "Hey! Wait a minute! We were supposed to be joking around. I was kidding. I loved that book; it's in my soul, and I want to talk to you about it for hours and hours and learn everything you know about it!" But, I didn't say that, of course. I didn't say anything. I watched him cross the road in the snow going toward Wentworth Hall.

What a stupid, lamebrain thing to do! Why couldn't I have told him that I'd read that entire monster of a book for the first time at Keewaydin the summer before? It had taken me nearly the whole summer. Just a few hours before I saw Mr. Leonard, I'd finished rereading the best parts, some out loud to Larry, poor bored jock that he was, who couldn't believe that any human being was physically capable of reading anything that long, especially when you could get some brain's complete notes on something like this for only a medium threat of bodily harm. No, instead, I tried to joke around with him. After all, I was used to joking around with Mr. Leonard. Why didn't he take it that way? Didn't he know I was joking? I was confused and didn't know what to make of it. I guessed that I'd picked a lousy time to joke around.

What happened next was much worse. Since I was sure I'd ace the *Moby-Dick* quiz, I did play bridge that very night in the buttroom of Wentworth Hall with Black Sam against two guys I didn't know very well. We'd started at the heady level of a penny-a-point and had gone up to the sweaty-palm level of ten cents a point, which meant even a moderately successful evening could easily produce two or three hundred dollars. I tried not to think about losing that much.

There were just the four of us in the buttroom quietly playing when the door flew open and a mob of seniors I didn't know burst in. A couple of big guys stood guard at the door and the son of a hugely rich tycoon and his cronies began unpacking two suitcases they'd brought along. Out came a half-sized mahogany and brass roulette wheel, a large green felt playing field and masses of plastic chips and plaques in a variety of colors. Soon the room was packed; the inaudible tom-toms of Exeter's amazing underground communications system, the equal of any prison's, had worked well. The Wentworth buttroom was the place to be. The rich guy, who acted as cool as a croupier at the Casino in Monte Carlo, didn't play at all—he was the house, the banker, as well as the croupier, and he did a tremendous business that night.

Although it was all pretty exciting, I really wanted none of it. I just wanted a quiet evening of bridge making some money. That was not to be—all the commotion killed any hope of a bridge game. I was worried that it might also bring in the authorities, and I wasn't even supposed to be in that room. Since the juices were flowing, I stayed to watch a bit until my fear of getting caught impelled me to grope through the crowd toward the single door out of there. As soon as I got to the door—in fact, I had my hand on the knob—it jerked open and suddenly I was staring at the enraged face of Chilson Leonard.

As he came through the door, his large body filling up the entire frame, Mr. Leonard reached out one thick, strong arm and grabbed me by the neck. At that very moment—I could hardly believe it—the goddamn little steel ball dropped into a slot on the roulette wheel, a voice yelled "Fifteen Black" and the groans of the losers almost drowned out the yelps of a couple of winners. Well, I thought that either Mr. Leonard was going to fall down and die twitching, choked with rage, right there and then, or that he would kill me by crushing my neck which was held fast in the clamp of his hand. I really didn't know which. Instead, although I'm sure he thought of both of those possibilities, and probably greatly preferred killing me, Mr. Leonard plunged through the crowd arm over arm, wielding me around like a machete to hack through the jumble of bodies. We wiped out at least five or six good-sized guys on the way to the other side of that room, which quickly smelled of human panic, mostly mine, as well as stale smoke.

By the time Mr. Leonard had punched his way through the crowd using me as his battering ram and reached the table, the green felt, chips, plaques, and even the mahogany wheel were all gone. Nothing was left, not even the suitcases. When we got there, four seniors were sitting at the table holding half-played bridge hands with a score sheet indicating that several hands had already been played. Another student hovered over one of the players like a buzzard, peered into his hand thoughtfully and looked quizzically at us as if we'd interrupted him.

Mr. Leonard, at least as bewildered as I was, looked all around, frantically searching for the evidence that he knew had to be there. Spotting nothing except innocent, blank stares and a few smirks, he started scratching his head with his right hand, looking completely befuddled. As he bent down trying to find the evidence looking through a forest of legs, someone began to laugh, a sort of choking chortle, as if he was trying not to. It was infectious, and a couple of others began to snigger, then more, until a lot of guys were standing there looking at Mr. Leonard and laughing at him in his obvious confusion and distress. A black cloud came over Leonard's face and his eyes became tiny burning coals almost hidden by the scowl that wrinkled his face. He clenched his teeth and bellowed with all of his considerable power: "Get out! Everyone—Get—The—Hell—Out—Of—Here—NOW!"

The laughing stopped and the room was empty almost before he'd finished speaking. In the stampede to the door, I was picked up and swept out like suds down the drain. Once outside, the panicked herd ran amok in all directions back to wherever they came from. I ran back up to my room, heart thumping, neck aching so bad that I thought it was seriously injured, aware now of bruises all over my body from being used as a blunt instrument, and aware, also, that a Major Event had just occurred in my life.

The next day, when my class took his *Moby-Dick* quiz, Mr. Leonard didn't say a single word to me and I didn't know what to say to him. Maybe the whole thing would blow over, I thought.

He could nail me for being in the buttroom, but maybe he doesn't want to. Maybe, he's still my pal. But, the day after that, two things happened that were not good. The first was that, as usual, Mr. Leonard distributed our *Moby-Dick* quiz papers with our grades circled in red. However, as was not his custom, he passed them out at random so that no one had his own quiz. Then he sat down at one end of the big wood table we all sat around and put his leather grade book out in front of him. He announced that he would read the name of each person in the class and directed that, after he'd read each person's name aloud, whoever held that person's quiz should pass it on to its owner after calling out the circled grade so that he could enter it in his grade book—in this way, he said, we could help him save time. The procedure seemed weird to us, but it was fine with me since I knew my stuff on *Moby-Dick* and was confident that I'd done a good job on the essay which wasn't on the symbolism of the white whale, as most everyone thought it would be, but on why Ishmael was the narrator. That was a really interesting question. So, I waited. My name was duly called after Booger Baxter's 78 was duly recorded. "Forty-two" lisped the no-name brain who had my quiz and had (sometimes) bested me before, clearly relishing the moment as he pushed my paper across the table to me. Then the process resumed. Wait a minute! I wanted to scream—42? How could that possibly be? I snatched my paper up from the table. Sure enough, there was a big "42" circled in red at the top with a comment scrawled down the side: "Unconvincing. Poor work. Disappointing." The last word was underlined twice.

Wow, I thought. This is really serious. This is my best course and I just can't afford to screw it up. What's happening?

I was still trying to sort out why I'd gotten a 42 on the quiz about an hour later when the Principal himself interrupted my Latin class and asked the teacher to excuse me so that I could join him in his office immediately. I'd never seen him do that before. In fact, I never saw the Principal much at all; he was always off campus somewhere, probably fundraising.

For me, the walk to the Principal's office was like James Cagney's walk to the hot seat in *Angels With Dirty Faces* snarling and undefeated. Me? I was jelly-limbed and wanted desperately to run away. I glanced furtively at the Principal trying to pick up some sign of what my future held. Wait a minute—how bad could it be to get a 42 on a quiz, anyway? Do they torture kids for that? I still didn't get it.

The Principal's profile looked just like the Old Man of the Mountain, a craggy face etched over eons by the elements on Cannon Mountain in the White Mountains of New Hampshire. He seemed just as big and unfeeling as that granite face, and didn't look like he was in the mood to do me any favors, even if he had known Dad at college.

When we reached the Principal's large office in Jeremiah Smith Hall, Mr. Leonard was already there waiting for us, standing behind a chair in one corner, glowering. The Principal told me to sit down in a wooden chair facing him across his desk, my back to Mr. Leonard. I had just about suppressed a cowardly compulsion to run away and was all set to launch into a strong defense of my record in English II, when the Principal began to speak.

"As you know, and now we know, too, there was gambling going on in Wentworth Hall the night before last, and, most likely, before then as well. We know that you know all about it and are involved in it. At the same time, Mr. Leonard has reported that your academic work—at least in English II—has recently become unacceptable. On top of those things, you were observed smoking in the buttroom in Wentworth, a place that is completely off limits to you, as you well know. For breaking the smoking rules, you are suspended from school for a period of one week, beginning immediately. Whether or not you will be permitted to return to school at the end of that week depends on what happens here. First, do you admit that you were smoking?"

"Sir, I admit that I have smoked sometimes, but I wasn't smoking that night. Honestly, I wasn't smoking then."

"So you admit breaking the rule against smoking. Next, were you involved in any way with this roulette business?"

"No, sir."

"Do you deny that there was a roulette wheel in the smoking room of Webster Hall the night before last?"

"No, sir."

"You had nothing to do with it?"

"Yes, sir; I mean, no, I didn't."

"Who did? Tell me who was responsible."

That's what he asked, no fooling. He was giving me the grisly choice between martyrdom and finking on popular, and much bigger, upperclassmen who could ruin my life at Exeter in any number of ways—a truly grisly situation and with only a few seconds to make a choice that I knew could haunt me forever. I groped for a way out.

"Sir, you can't ask me that. I just can't do that, as much as I want to stay here at school."

Things took another strange turn then. The Principal raised

his bushy white eyebrows and his craggy, wrinkled frown smoothed out into something approaching a benign smile. At the same time, Chilson Leonard pounced.

"You smart-ass, pipsqueak, little son-of-a-bitch; you'd better tell us who it was or so help me God I'll see that whatever feeble chance you have of getting into college—any college, anywhere —ends right here!"

Wow! This is bad news, I thought. I believed absolutely in his power to make good on his threat but was completely confused by his attack on me, his pal! Not daring even to look at Mr. Leonard's enraged face, I kept my eyes riveted on the Principal as his smile faded at the ferocity of Leonard's onslaught. He raised his hand to stop Leonard, and once again frowning and deeply serious, spoke quietly to me.

"I understand how you could feel you can't inform on other students. I do understand that. While I do know that it is a difficult choice for you to make, you should also know that not telling us might well have consequences you can't foresee now. It could affect your whole future. However, you alone are responsible for placing yourself in this unhappy position and so you are solely responsible for the consequences, whatever they may be. Do you understand that?"

"Yes, sir."

"The question stands. Who was responsible? What's your decision?"

"I just can't do it, sir. I'm really sorry. I wish I could," I blurted out, staring between my legs at the rug on the floor, unable to look him in the eye. My ears were on fire.

A full minute went by before his swivel chair squeaked as he leaned back. The Principal scratched his craggy chin. "Maybe that's the right decision. You may never know. I can't speak for the faculty, however. I don't know how they'll feel about it. Maybe, some will agree with your choice. I do know that others will disagree, maybe even very, very strongly."

Leonard was stunned. "What the hell are you talking about? I want you to make him tell us NOW or I want you to throw him the hell out—out—out of here! He's a worthless conniving weasel!" I was shocked to hear him shout and I shrank and became as small as I possibly could. "He's a cheater! I know he cheats. He's nothing but a goddamn, smart-ass wiseacre and he is going out of here on the balls of his ass, and if you don't do it, I sure as hell will."

Later, the Principal told me to get whatever I needed together and be off the campus on the way home as soon as possible. He would call me at home to discuss my suspension with me and my father. I stopped by the art gallery to see Mrs. Baker before I left. She told me that she'd heard there had been a faculty meeting at lunchtime and that most of the Faculty had disagreed with Leonard's recommendation to expel me—he didn't have any evidence of my cheating—and voted instead to suspend me for one week for smoking as the Principal had suggested. As for the gambling, they gave the Principal the right to extend my suspension for as long as he decided, even through the end of the year. As a sop to Leonard, they also decreed that, if and when I returned to school, I would be placed on academic and social probation for the rest of the school year, which meant that bad marks or the slightest infraction of the most minor rule would send me packing. Chilson Leonard was not satisfied.

I don't remember the trip home. I'm sure that no one drove up to take me home, so I must have taken the train to Boston, then switched to South Station to get the New York train to Grand Central, then switched again to take the commuter train to Ardsley-on-Hudson. I don't remember any of it. I was stunned and confused. I do remember Dad coming home from the office my first night at home and telling me that "Salty" had called him. That happened every night during my first days of banishment from Exeter. Dad would tell me about the telephone conversation he'd had with the Principal that day, although it was pretty much the same every day. Mr. Saltonstall wouldn't give up trying to find a way to persuade me to turn informer because Mr. Leonard still wanted the name of the ringleader and was continuing to press the Principal to extract it from me. Dad became more and more convinced that the best thing—in fact, the only thing—for me was to tell them what they wanted to know. The more certain he became, the more certain I became that I shouldn't do it.

"Doncha see?" Dad asked. "Leonard's not going to give up. You know you've got to go back to his class if they ever let you go back—it's too late to switch. You know that. So, what's it going to be like for you there, with Leonard mad as hell at you?"

"Maybe he'll get over it?" I suggested, a little weakly.

"Don't be silly. That just isn't going to happen. I don't know what Leonard will do, but I'm sure that your future—for the rest of the year with Leonard and, maybe, for the rest of your life—will be a lot better if you give them a name, doncha see? Just one name?"

Whatever Dad said and however much he persisted, I didn't

see how he could be right, although I understood that he wanted me to go back and finish at Exeter very much. Sure, it would probably be a lot better for me in Mr. Leonard's class, but what about with my friends? What about Larry? What would he, and Seth and Bradford and Booger—what would they all think? My bridge bunch wouldn't speak to me much less let me play with them anymore. And, what about the seniors who would probably get expelled? And their friends? Exeter was a really big place and bad things happened to kids sometimes—I'd heard a kid was found hanging in a bathroom once not long before. Everyone said it was a suicide, but maybe he ratted on a bunch of seniors—who knows? The faculty could never keep close track of all the kids in a school as big as Exeter. And, how would it possibly be better for me for the rest of my life knowing that I'd turned traitor to save my own ass? How could I live with that?

Dad also called Mrs. Baker and tried to get her to help. She said she didn't like Mr. Leonard a lot—no one did, she said—but what could she do? She also said that everybody was afraid of Chilson Leonard, including herself.

Dad got frantic. Red-faced after a few of his nightly whiskey and waters, he implored me, either to do what Mr. Leonard wanted and give him the guy's name or give the name to the Principal. In fact, he offered to tell the Principal himself, if I would tell him. He said he'd tell Mr. Saltonstall that he'd made me divulge the name against my will so I couldn't be blamed. We argued about it, or rather he whined at me about it, a lot. "Doncha see the pickle you've gotten yourself into this time? Doncha see that you've just got to tell them? Doncha see that? Why don't you just go ahead and tell them, for Heaven's sake?"

I told him I was sure he was trying to help, but I didn't think that any of his ideas would work out too well for me, so I'd better not.

At the end of my first week of suspension, Principal Saltonstall told Dad that I could come back to school, but that, since I'd be on probation for the rest of the year, I might not make it through —if I did anything wrong, anything at all, I'd get bounced. Did he and I understand that? Dad said he understood and would make damn sure I understood. Then Dad called Mrs. Baker and asked her to look out for me. She said she'd do that and asked me to come to dinner at her house the night I got back. Mom and Dad both put me on the train at the little Victorian train station at Ardsley-on-Hudson. Standing on the platform, Dad was grim. "Buckle down, stop smoking, obey all the rules and keep your nose clean," he said. "Maybe, just maybe, you can survive this unfortunate episode after all. I certainly hope so."

MY GRADES ON the weekly papers and quizzes Mr. Leonard gave us during the rest of the Spring Term were mostly in the 30's and 40's, but I even got a 26 on an essay on *The Scarlet Letter*—just about my favorite book of the entire year. Every one of those incredible, humiliating grades were announced by someone else around that big wood table which became more and more like a torture rack for me. More and more I began to wonder if I could take it. Would I get a migraine that would never go away? Would I crack up and have a nervous breakdown, whatever that was? Maybe I really was stupid after all? Maybe, I'd already lost it and everyone but me knew it.

When it first began, my pals and the other kids in the class saw clearly what was happening. They knew full well that my low marks were not legitimate and hated Mr. Leonard with me. Then, slowly, they changed. They began to treat me as if I really was an idiot. At the end, they all did—even my best friends, Larry, Bingham, Bradford and Booger. I don't know what Downey thought; he called everyone an idiot all the time. Earlier in the year, when I was a rising star, they'd want to know what I had to say about the books we were reading in class. We'd meet before tests to bone up and, maybe, try to dope out what the questions would be. I was pretty good at that, as good or better than anybody else. Now, they still met together sometimes, but I wasn't asked to be part of it. Long before school ended, they and all the other kids in the class stopped caring what I thought. After all, I was getting the lowest English II marks in the history of Exeter. I began to believe, and at the end was convinced, that I had nothing to offer. I didn't blame them for not including me in the prep sessions. What could I tell them? Maybe they were afraid I'd give them a bum steer or something, as if whatever infection I had was catching.

Once, after only about a month of torture, I raised my hand to answer a question I knew cold about one of Poe's short stories. There was a groan, as if the other kids were saying, "Why bother? We don't care what you've got to say." So I put my hand down. I didn't think Mr. Leonard was going to call on me anyway. He'd stopped doing that right at the beginning. He ignored me completely. It was as if I wasn't in the room. Maybe, I began to think, those awful grades were, after all, the best I could do. Maybe I had a brain tumor. I stopped reading. I stopped hanging around with Bradford and the other guys or going to the Grill with Larry. In fact, I pretty much stopped doing anything except listening to my records—that is, when I didn't have a migraine. I wasn't hungry and missed a lot of meals, especially breakfast, since I got up late every morning. While I was able to make most of my classes, I didn't talk to anybody for days at a time.

IN LATE MAY, Bob came to the big lacrosse game with Andover, Exeter's oldest rival. He was a junior at Harvard majoring in Government and still trying to think of something to do other than go to law school and follow Dad—and our grandfather, uncle and even an aunt—into becoming a lawyer. He'd fallen for a girl from Radcliffe I hadn't met and seemed upset at himself that she hadn't come with him to the game because by the time he'd asked her, she already had a date. He was like that. He'd wait forever to get up his nerve to call a girl and then do it at the last possible minute. When she was busy, he'd get all upset about it. Still, it seemed that chasing her was keeping his spirits up and not letting him depress himself too much about his future, so I tried to keep him talking about her, but it didn't work.

"How's it going with your English teacher, little brother?" he asked since he knew a little about my problem, I guessed mostly from Mom who probably talked to him about me as if I had a terminal brain tumor. I'd bet he'd even ask her sometimes "how's the patient doing?" as if I was sick.

"Not so good, Bob. Not good at all, in fact. I don't know what game he's playing with me, but I'm losing." I told him about the 26 on my paper about *The Scarlet Letter.*

"How can he do that? I mean why not a 37 or a 22.5? What makes it a 26? Did he tell you?"

"No. He doesn't explain his grades. Just writes comments like 'shows no preparation' or 'unoriginal.' The latest was something like 'consistent with your recent poor work—I suggest you read the book'—that was with a 35 he gave me on a paper on a book I'd really worked on."

"What a bastard! Do you talk to him?"

"No, not really. I can't. I mean he won't talk to me. He ignores me. I'm lucky to get a grunt if I ask him something, so I don't ask anymore. At least he doesn't call on me in class anymore either. It's like I'm not there. I'm a non-person."

"Want me to speak to him? I know him a little. I never had him in English, thank God, but I remember him. Think it could help?"

"I don't know. Maybe. It's hard to see how anything could hurt."

"Okay, but you are working hard, aren't you? You promise me you're not screwing off, if I'm going to speak to him," Bob said. I told him that I was working as hard as when I'd gotten great marks, but if he didn't want to speak to Mr. Leonard he didn't have to. He must have forgotten or decided against it or something, because he went back to Harvard that afternoon without talking to Mr. Leonard, who was also there at the game, sitting alone as usual.

IT WAS HARD to get up in the morning. Larry had begun to get up very early, get all his books and things together and leave the room before I was even awake. He'd stay away all day, I guess because he knew that, if I wasn't actually in a class, I'd be in our room. It was usually just before ten o'clock at night when he'd come back to our room, get his toothbrush and go down the hall to brush his teeth. He'd undress and get into bed right after that. Maybe he'd ask me how it was going, or what I did that day. By the beginning of May, he didn't talk to me much at all. It wasn't because he was mad at me—I hadn't done anything to make him mad. It was like I wasn't there. I think I made him feel bad, so it was better to pretend I wasn't there. And, I know I made him feel bad—I couldn't help it. I made everyone feel bad. I felt awful all the time.

Sometimes, when Larry had gone in the morning and if I didn't have a class right away, I'd pick up a book and try to read. After looking at a page for what felt like about a minute but was closer to half an hour, I'd realize that I'd read the same sentence over and over and still didn't understand anything I'd read. I'd try to focus, but it would happen again and again. So, I stopped trying to read and would shut my eyes for a minute. Several times I didn't wake up until late in the afternoon, risking the wrath of the teachers whose classes I'd missed. When that happened for the first time, I panicked, thinking that I was surely about to get thrown out of school. I went to the infirmary and was able to cough and wheeze my way into an excuse. As time went on and I kept coming into the infirmary, sometimes with a migraine and sometimes without anything specific, the nurse caught on that I was going through something bad. She asked me what was wrong, but I didn't know. I just felt bad and didn't want to do anything. I just wanted to go to sleep for a hundred years. Maybe I had mono, the nurse thought, until she took a blood test.

I did manage to show up for most of my classes, but they were like a blur. I tried to be invisible and never said anything in class.

I guess it worked because none of my teachers called on me. I began to think that maybe they all knew something. The word was out that I was so stupid that it was useless to ask me anything.

One night when the end of the school year was only a few weeks away and after Larry had gone to bed without talking to me and our lights were out, he asked me what I was going to do during the summer. Did I have any plans? I was lying on top of my bed still dressed, except for my shoes, which was the way I sometimes went to sleep. I was looking out our window at the dark trees and the black night. No, I said, I didn't have any plans. It seemed strange to me that I didn't have any plans, but there it was—I hadn't thought of anything beyond the day I would finally leave Exeter.

THE LAST CLASS of English II for the year took place the day after I'd meant to listen to a speech by President Eisenhower on the radio about Senator Joseph McCarthy. But, I stayed in my room and forgot about the speech even though I wanted to hear Ike throttle McCarthy, who was pretty creepy—another Mr. Leonard. In fact, I was sure Mr. Leonard secretly admired McCarthy and would have been great at accusing innocent people of being Commies. On the day of that last class, most of us could hardly wait for the summer vacation to start. I, of course, was more eager than any of them to end the hideous ordeal I had come to accept as a natural part of my life. I was now used to the torture rack, convinced that I deserved it. I thought I was where I was supposed to be. I deserved what was happening to me.

The last class began with Mr. Leonard passing out a sheet of paper to each of us listing our grades on each quiz and paper

he'd given us during the second half of the year and then a sepa-
rate number which was our grade for the entire first half. Next,
he told us to add up all the numbers for this term and divide
by 22, the total number of grades we'd received on quizzes and
tests during the term. Then, we should add the result to the
first term's grade and divide by two to get our final mark for
the entire year. I did all that, finding that my Spring Term average was 31 and when that was added to my Fall Term's 87, my
final grade for the year was a mathematically inescapable 59. I
did it again—same answer. I just sat there and looked at it—59.
It was the biggest number I'd seen in a long time. It didn't look
too bad.

Mr. Leonard called on each kid to announce his own final
grade. He had his leather grade book open in front of him. When
it was my turn, I whispered "59." He looked up from the grade
book, smiled at me, and said flatly but loudly: "So you flunk for
the year." Then, after pausing to look at the other kids around
the table, he called out the next name. None of my friends or
the other kids in the class said anything to me. In fact, none of
them even looked at me as we left Mr. Leonard's classroom and
I shuffled back toward my room.

Dad and Mom were waiting for me outside Webster Hall to begin the long drive home. When I told them I'd flunked English
with a 59 average, Mom got teary and Dad got all worked up.

"Dammit, I knew something like this was going to happen!"
He said he was going to do something about it. What could he
do, change my grade? Maybe I deserved it. Anyhow, he grabbed
me by the arm and tugged me along with him. We went to the
art gallery and found Mrs. Baker taking a picture off the wall.

Dad made me tell her what had happened and then he went at her, walking back and forth in the middle of the gallery, stroking the back of his head.

"Isn't there something you can do?" He seemed to be begging. "There must be something you can do or someone you can call. You owe me that much, don't you?"

Of course, there was nothing Mrs. Baker could do. She said that all she did is manage the art gallery. Who would listen to her about what happened in an English class? In Chilson Leonard's English class? I thought she was going to cry the way Dad was leaning on her. He had an awful grimace on his face and he told her again that he thought she owed him, that she just had to try to do something, doncha see? She didn't know what to do. Dad didn't know what Mr. Leonard was like. She could lose her job. She just stood there, looking down at the floor. She was pretty upset. He was in a frenzy. My stomach was in a knot. Leave the poor lady alone, I wished almost out loud. It's my fault, not hers.

When it was clear he was getting nowhere with Mrs. Baker, Dad charged over to the Principal's office towing me along and found that it was as if we were expected. Dad whined at his old friend, Mr. Saltonstall, too, but it didn't work with him either. The Principal said he was powerless; he had no authority to change any teacher's grades. Leonard's mark would have to stand. Since passing English II was required, my only choices were to go to another school or to take and pass it in summer school. The summer school English II course would be taught that year by my pal, the Master of Wentworth Hall.

I calculated that the long trip home from Exeter would take

about sixteen thousand, two hundred seconds, and each one of them oozed by like a slow drip from a leaky faucet. Dad drove, of course. He stared at the broken white line in the middle of the highway in front of him, blinking sometimes when we passed over the joints of the concrete slabs, kerthunk, kerthunk, ker-thunk. Mom sat in the middle with her jaws clenched instead of her knuckles. She also stared straight ahead, not looking at anything in particular. I sat in the Death Seat wondering if they would ever say anything to me. I was tensed up too, but since they weren't talking, I just looked out as big, leafy green trees, and some cows now and then, flickered by in the hot afternoon sun by my half-open window.

Outside, the countryside shimmered in the heat of the June day as we passed from southern New Hampshire through the middle of Massachusetts and Connecticut into New York State —Duchess, Putnam and, at last, Westchester County. Inside the car, it was different. It was hot and my shirt was drenched and stuck to the back of the seat, but my hands felt icy cold. The car was filled with the moist, clammy fog I hated. I was shivering.

I knew I'd broken something—a pretty nice something, a big and expensive something—maybe, the most important thing in the world. I imagined a perfect crystal wineglass. It had shat-tered and couldn't be put back together. I'd broken it, I knew that, and so did they, but no one said so. This thing I'd broken was just there, lying there right in front of us in pieces. We could all see it. I knew that Dad thought that if we didn't talk about something, it wasn't really there and that Mom was afraid of saying anything that would probably make him mad and growl "drop it." So, I knew Dad wouldn't talk about it and was pretty sure Mom wouldn't either, but for once I wished she would talk, even if that would provoke Dad. He probably wanted to scream at me, but I knew he probably wouldn't scream, even if he was furious. He wouldn't let himself do that. Instead, he would croak, as if he was strangling, and out would come a singsong whine as sour as curdled milk. My hands were freezing.

I looked out the window at the trees whizzing by and remembered myself standing alone in front of Dunbar Hall less than two years before, when Mom and Dad had dropped me off at Exeter. In my mind's eye, I saw myself watching as this same green Ford station wagon with wood panels drove away from Dunbar and stopped for a moment at a sign that read "Phillips Exeter Academy, Founded 1781." Would the car turn back? No, it eased out through the stone gates into the main street, slowly picked up speed and disappeared down the straight black macadam road. I watched as the car grew smaller and smaller and then disappeared. I remembered exactly how time had stopped for me at that moment as my parents left. Everything in the universe had scemed frozen, locked for a moment. I remembered how much I'd wanted to go home.

Now, almost two years later, I was going home.

Chapter Six

By the end of July, Mom had taken me to visit four schools in various parts of New England that she thought might, possibly, accept me. I hated the first three of them, which were too ghastly, even if Mom and Dad thought I got what was coming to me, what I deserved. Clearly, they didn't believe that I'd gotten a raw deal. Or, at least, they never said so.

I began the tour of the first three schools doubting that any of them, or maybe any school anywhere, would ever accept me. I ended it hoping that none would. I didn't fit in any of them. The first school seemed to be no more than a bunch of cabins in the woods. It looked like the summer camp in New Hampshire I'd gone to when I was ten. It was small and very progressive. When Mom heard the dorms were co-ed, she tuned out and we left before I'd even had a tour of the campus. The next one, in northwestern Connecticut, was also really small. It had tiny little wooden chairs with tiny little writing arms attached, neatly lined up in each tiny little classroom. My soul shrank at the thought of spending two years like Gulliver surrounded by the Lilliputians who could fit into that furniture. Later, when I told her about that school, Betty, one of our tiny Irish maids, tried to make me feel better: "Little people aren't all so bad," she said with a sly leprechaun grin. The third school was founded by a nineteenth century evangelist. The Admissions Director showed Mom and me into his dark wood-paneled office and sat down behind his desk facing us with his hands pressed together as if he was praying. There was a window directly behind him and the afternoon sun blazed in my eyes. I couldn't look at him. But, from his attitude, I knew it didn't matter. He was sure that whatever I'd done at Exeter was ugly and unhealthy and it was his job to make sure that the student body at his school stayed healthy. He started in by asking me if I'd "…learned anything from being thrown out of Exeter." Sure, I remember thinking. I learned to keep as far away as possible from people like you. But, I didn't say that. There was no humor in him. I couldn't wait to leave that place. But, where would I go? Maybe, I had no future.

I KNEW MOM worried a lot about me. Before the cocktail hour transformed her from a sane and normal person into a disgusting Cubist abstraction, she was bright and cheery and thought of lots of things to keep me busy and my spirits up, but it didn't work so well. I moped around the house, depressing the dogs, the cat and even the tropical fish. I watched them for hours and noticed when they began to swim sluggishly around the big tank in our "den," which was what Mom renamed our refurbished playroom when Bob and I outgrew it. Then, one by one, the kissing gouramis, tetras, swordtails and the others died, turning belly up until all that was left of a thriving population was a single, huge, ugly catfish which spent most of its time sucking debris off the bottom and vacuuming algae off the sides of the tank. I hated the big catfish and wondered how it, alone, could survive. Sometimes, I wondered how I, alone, could survive since, after all, I had no future. I also had no driver's license.

I had always been a bit melancholy, but having no future was something else again. That was new. Before I left Exeter, I could still clearly see the family path, well blazed by Dad, Bob, our cousin Tim and other relatives; but it was now closed to me. It had suddenly taken a nasty turn for me, into unfamiliar territory. Did it go up into Connecticut where I'd have to serve a two-year sentence in the Little House, cohabiting with tiny little classmates, scrunched into kiddy furniture? Or, did it take me to the religious school where I'd spend the next two years on my knees in prayer exorcising the evil inside me? I couldn't see myself at either place. Worse, what would happen to me after prep school? Every time my future came up, Dad made it sound as if it wasn't important. I really didn't have a future. No wonder I was depressed.

No wonder I stole my mother's little yellow Nash Rambler. I needed adventure, and, on one afternoon in midsummer, got more than I wanted. Dad and Mom had gone somewhere for the long weekend over the Fourth of July. They left in the big green Ford station wagon early on Friday morning. Mom told me that her sister, my Aunt Mary, and her husband, Uncle Lloyd, were on their way out from the City to spend the weekend at our house. She hoped I wouldn't be lonesome and they'd be home on Monday afternoon. No problem, I'd said. I'll be fine.

Now a house devoid of parents, even for a few hours, was as attractive to my neighborhood rat pack as Brigitte Bardot, and a whole lot more accessible. Within minutes, the usual bunch of kids I'd grown up with, home from Choate, Andover and nearby Hackley, were in my house, raiding the refrigerator for Pepsis, making telephone calls to people named Lyons who were instructed to call for an urgent message at a number that turned out to be the Bronx Zoo's, or urging the several listed Clapps to see their doctors immediately. Within an hour, there were kids everywhere, getting into the drawers of the big chest in our living room and finding old photographs to pass around and chuckle at, looking behind the books on all the shelves and discovering pure gold in the form of a very clinical, but illustrated, marriage manual even I didn't know was there. Unfortunately, the drawings, especially the scientific cross sections of the vagina and ovaries, were pretty disappointing.

At the peak, there were over twenty of them, some I'd never seen before, all between about thirteen and sixteen. Most of them had their bikes, but three of the oldest had cars. When the group spontaneously decided that the delights of my house had been exhausted and it was time to move on to the local Dairy Queen five miles away, twenty kids into three cars did not go.

I could almost hear Mom's little yellow Rambler calling me into taking her out for a little spin. What the hell, I thought, no one will ever know since I'll have the little bug back before my aunt and uncle arrive and, while I was hardly an experienced driver, it never occurred to me that anything would happen; such was my thinking. Four of the leftovers and I crammed into the Rambler and headed off with me at the wheel, charged up with a powerful sense of adventure, singing along with the radio at top blast "Sh-boom, Sh-boom, ya da da da da da da."

On the way back, my passengers hanging their legs and arms out of the windows and screaming obscenities at passing cars, I came to a street at the top of a long, sloping hill which dead-ended at a T-intersection with Route 9, the main drag through that part of Westchester County, heavily traveled by cars and trucks in both directions at some times. I put my foot on the brakes. Nothing happened. I stomped on the pedal as hard as I could, pushing it all the way to the floorboards. Still nothing happened. The speedometer showed that we were doing about twenty-five and had only a few hundred yards before the intersection. Cars and trucks were whizzing by in pretty heavy traffic. I tried the emergency hand brake. It came up in my hand easily, without any effect. I didn't know how to stop! I looked on both sides of the road for a place to crash. I didn't have my foot on the accelerator, so we weren't gaining speed but we weren't stopping either. Trees lined the road—big, old, stout trees with no room between them to turn the Rambler safely. My pals were now screaming things like "Slow down the fucking car, stupid" and other helpful advice, which stopped when they all realized that we were in really serious trouble, heading straight for disaster.

The Rambler shot out into the intersection, just missing a panel truck and listed as I made a hard left into the farthest lane going south, righted itself and, suddenly, I was looking straight ahead down Route 9. There were no other cars in my lane for half a mile. My friends were wild with shock and fear—they'd

Dad mugging with unknown friends in the early 1930's

A portrait Mom had taken in 1946. From left: Bob,
age eleven, my mother age forty, me, age six

A portrait of Dad taken
for his fiftieth birthday in
December, 1951

Mom and Dad at Dad's 45th
Reunion of the Class of 1924
at Harvard, 1969

Bob, after he joined the New
York law firm of Sullivan &
Cromwell, 1960

Dr. Ferdinand Kertess with
daughter Barbara at Jewelle's
and my wedding, 1962

William G. Saltonstall,
Principal of Exeter, 1954

Class picture (detail) from *The PEAN*, 1954. Second row:
Larry Fraser, first from left; myself, fourth from left; Peter
Benchley, fifth from left

Chilson H. Leonard, my
English II teacher, 1954

Drawing by Bruce Davidson

The main entrance to the Academy Building at Exeter
with inscription: *Huc Venite, Pueri, ut Viri Sitis*
("Come hither boys so that ye may become men")

Ford Hall at Williston Academy from the school's
yearbook, *The Log,* 1957

My senior picture at Williston, 1957

A serious me as Chairman of the Graduation Committee at Williston taken in spring of 1957. Peter Revson, on my right, had just completed most of the work on his own memoir, *Speed with Style*, about his experiences as a world-class racing driver when he was killed during a practice run before the South African Grand Prix in Johannesburg in 1974 at the age of thirty-five. On my left is John Houghton, a CPA and jazz pianist in San Francisco whose first CD was released in 2002. Arthur Pellman, standing directly behind me, retired from teaching English in the New York City public schools in order to pursue his acting career.

Phillips Stevens, Headmaster of Williston
Academy in his office, mid-1950's

George McCall Maxwell
September 21, 1917 – January 30. 1957

The first photograph of Jewelle and me taken on one
of our first dates at a coin-operated photo machine in
White Plains, New York in the fall of 1957.

seen things I'm glad I didn't. The man driving the panel truck had seen us too late to do anything and had thrown his arms in front of his head, anticipating an inevitable crash that we must have missed only by inches.

Still, I had plenty to think about. Avoiding that crash was one thing, even a miracle, perhaps, but what happens now? I was on a main road, still moving pretty fast and without any brakes or any idea of how to stop the car. The speed was falling off slightly. I turned off the engine, which helped a bit. So did turning it on again and changing gears. What would happen if I jammed it into reverse? I was sure I didn't want to find out, but it might be better than crashing head on into something. We continued to slow down as the stone pillars that marked the turn for Ardsley Avenue, the road leading past my house, came into view. Could I make that turn and then take a quick left and whip into the driveway of my house? What then? Should I total the Rambler right on our front porch? My own house? Good Grief! My parents! Aunt Mary and Uncle Lloyd! I hadn't thought of how in the world I could ever explain all this to them; what could I possibly say? What incredible lie could I come up with to explain how Mom's favorite car got totaled on our own front porch? Better smash it up on a tree and die!

My instinct for self-preservation must have taken over just then because, I automatically made a quick right turn off Route 9 onto Ardsley Avenue and then another sharp left turn into my short driveway. The car had slowed a lot as a result of all the turns and inertia and I just hung on as it headed straight into its place in the garage and hit the back wall—thunk—and stalled. Thank God, the back wall didn't give way. I'd made it.

I tried to start the car up to move it back, but it wouldn't start, so we pushed it away from the wall to survey the damage. Not too much was apparent on the outside, except the bumper was pushed back a lot and there was something dripping from under the hood making a big puddle on the concrete floor. "Boy, are you gonna get it," suggested one of my co-conspirators helpfully. "I'm getting outa here," said Bert, who was just about my best friend at home, as he fled with the others, leaving me to face the music alone. I could hardly blame them, but still missed being able to rehash this amazing adventure with them.

By the time Aunt Mary and Uncle Lloyd arrived, I hadn't figured out an enormous lie, so I didn't say anything. They lolled around the house all weekend, read a lot, took a few walks, didn't drink much, and never went near the car. When Mom and Dad came home late that Monday afternoon, my aunt and uncle had already taken a train back to the City. It was not until the following morning that Mom discovered something was wrong with her Rambler when she went out to take it somewhere and, of course, it wouldn't start. She kept plugging away, thinking she'd flooded the carburetor, but gave up when the battery died. In a very black mood, she called Al, the mechanic at our local garage, and asked for help. Al came later that afternoon, examined the car carefully and with growing amazement. He reported that he didn't know how it could have happened, but the radiator was smashed and, maybe, the engine block was cracked—he'd have to take a closer look at the garage where he would have the car towed.

That night at the dinner table Dad and Mom talked about something for once. What to do about the car? Surely, Dad said,

Uncle Lloyd had wrecked the car and hadn't had the guts or the courtesy to tell them about it and apologize. He blamed it on Mom's Irish blood—everyone in her family except her mother drank too much. How could anyone be so inconsiderate or even so stupid to leave without a word when, obviously, the deed had to come to light sometime? Dad wanted to call Uncle Lloyd right away and suggest they go shopping together for a new car with Lloyd's meager wallet. Mom nixed that approach by saying that they could never afford that. Maybe, she said, they were so ashamed and embarrassed that they couldn't face what they'd done; Mom would call Aunt Mary and try to pry what had happened out of her, although they both agreed that what must have happened was, of course, that Lloyd did it. He was known to take a drink from time to time to keep Aunt Mary company, and she was a world-class guzzler. Aunt Mary didn't know how to drive, being a thoroughly citified person. Uncle Lloyd must have gotten stewed to the gills and run the car into the back wall of the garage. Most likely, he'd gotten so stiff he couldn't even remember doing it.

Of course, I listened to all that and didn't contribute much to the discussion. At one point, Dad asked me if they went out at night. Gee, I wasn't around all the time, so they could have, I said. Did they drink an awful lot, Mom asked me as if she might be guilty of inflicting an unforgettable trauma on her wholesome son who had enough problems of his own just then? Well…I looked at the ceiling and then out the window wistfully.

Dad finally decided that there was no point in trying to persuade dumb, poorly-heeled Uncle Lloyd that, obviously, he'd gotten so drunk that he couldn't even remember taking our car, let alone crashing it into the wall of the garage. Lloyd couldn't afford to buy us a new car, so, Dad just dropped it and, as far as I know, never raised the subject again. He just stuffed his anger somewhere where it joined the other poisons that ate at him.

I didn't feel good about letting Uncle Lloyd take the blame, but, what the hell, I was an outlaw and had no future. But, that cockiness soon dissolved. What in the world was I doing? I didn't know how to drive well enough to have taken the car out that way. Did I have some kind of death wish? Was I really trying to kill myself when I turned on the gas two years before?

I wondered if Mom suspected the truth and found a way to steer Dad away from it. She was good at that, having deflected many probes into her drinking. Perhaps, she remembered, as I sure did when we were talking about the Rambler, that Dad's seething, whining sullenness might sometime boil over into open, uncontrollable rage and violence. It didn't happen then, but it was always a lurking possibility we kept in the back of our minds ever since he'd hit Bob a few years before. Bob had refused to do something Dad had asked him to do—I think it was to pick up some glasses and Pepsi bottles in the den when we went in to the dinner table. Bob said he'd do it after dinner. Dad said to do it now. Bob said he thought that was dumb. It didn't seem like that huge a deal, but Dad's hands trembled and his face turned purple as he backed Bob against a wall and socked him with a closed fist on the side of his head, stunning him and knocking him down. Mom and I were right there, watching. I couldn't believe it. Dad had hit Bob and knocked him down. The dirty bastard!

I don't think any of us understood what had made Dad go crazy that one time—for it was the only time Dad ever actually struck anybody—but we never talked about it. I never forgot about it either.

I squirmed in torment through the inquest into the death of the Rambler at the dinner table that night, sure that my face would betray my guilt or that my body language would scream it out. Somehow, I got through it, as I got through a thousand other dinners at that table, a place none of us wanted to be. I don't think we even wanted to see each other, much less eat a meal together, but we did it every night at seven-thirty sharp.

During the daytime, before my Night Mother emerged from the gin, Mom did a lot of good things. Without telling a soul, she began playing the piano three times a week for disabled veterans still confined more than a decade after the War to a VA hospital near Peekskill, at least an hour's drive away. She had been going there for almost a month before I asked her what she did on those afternoons. She also played at St. Faith's House, a Catholic home for unwed mothers in Tarrytown, an old converted Victorian mansion that was sometimes the target of intolerant and hostile townspeople.

In fact, she did a lot of things with her time but told no one, as if no one would care. I understood why she thought so, since Dad scorned whatever she did. "Don't bother me with your foolish activities," Dad seemed to be saying in every way he knew how: "You are incapable of doing anything interesting or important." How wrong he was. I cared. I was really proud of her sneaking out of the house to play for disabled vets. Her face lit up when she told me how they sang the old songs she played and loved her visits. And, how desperate the poor young girls at St. Faith's were, having their babies all alone only to have them taken away and put up for adoption and usually having been thrown out of their own homes by their "loving" parents. But, I also wished that Mom was different.

THE LAST SCHOOL on Mom's agenda for me to look at was Williston Academy in Easthampton, Massachusetts, which I'd never heard of before. We didn't talk to anyone in the Admissions Department as we had at the other schools. Instead, our appointment was with the Headmaster, Phillips Stevens, in his office.

"Call me Phil," he said, but I knew I wouldn't. He was too formal for that. He was pretty tall—well over six feet—and had black hair flecked with gray. His round steel glasses magnified his eyes and made him seem amazed when he looked at you. The look in his eyes was intense; he was burning with passion for this school. After talking to me about the school for about half an hour, during which he never once mentioned Exeter, Mr. Stevens seemed excited that I might even consider coming to Williston.

"I think you'd like being here at Williston and I'm sure that Williston would like to have you here," he said. "I want you here and hope you decide to come."

He never asked what had happened to me at Exeter! This Headmaster was asking me to come to his school without even a look-see at my loathsome condition. That was enough for me. I was going to Williston Academy. I was shown around the campus by a student, but I was in a fog and saw only good things— the pretty campus with the kind of red brick buildings I was used to including the gym with a swimming pool where Williston swimmers had set many prep school records. I didn't really see anything and didn't ask any questions. I'd already said yes.

WHEN I NEXT saw Dr. Kertess, he was beside himself. "Vhat iss de matter vit you, Bumppo? Vy didn't you pop this crazyman Leonard in de noze? How can your fahter let dis terrible ting happen to you?" He was so upset that it was hard to discuss the whole thing rationally with him. I'd gone to see Dr. Kertess thinking I'd have a quiet, deep intellectual analysis of my "problem" with Chilson Leonard, and, maybe, get some new insight or perspective on it from that man of great experience who had suffered greatly himself from another, and vastly greater, sort of insanity. Sure. But, here he was, pacing around his huge living room in a rage almost tearing what was left of his wispy white hair out. I had to comfort him.

"I'm not sure Exeter was the place for me anyway. I wasn't too happy there. Maybe Mr. Leonard did me a favor—in disguise, for sure, but still a favor?"

"Maybe so, but dat's beside de point question. Vhat he did to you vas criminal! He tried to rob you of your self-respect – maybe de vorst ting one human bean can do to another. He should be shot!"

I told him I didn't think that was going to happen and that it was more likely that Mr. Leonard would get a promotion. Why would a school keep someone like Mr. Leonard on the faculty at all, he kept asking, and what did Dad think about all this? I told him about Dad's pushing me to tell them the senior's name and how he thought I'd made the wrong choice by not doing that. As a result, I had no future. I had no one other than myself to blame for that and now had to face the consequences.

Dr. Kertess composed himself and said quietly: "I don't vant to be critical of your fahter, but I tink he's wrong. I tink you made de right choice—and how you had de guts to stand up to dem de vay you did, I don't know. I do know dat you haff a great future. You haff strength lots of people don't haff to tink for yourself and to haff confidence in yourself. You used to haff dat confidence—I saw it myself sitting right here vit you many times. Vhat you need now is to get back on de right track and discover dat confidence again. Your heart needs to know you did de right ting, no matter vhat your fahter or de people at your old school say. I hope dat vill happen at your new school—tell me, vhat iss your new school?"

I told him I'd been around to see a bunch of schools and had decided to go to Williston Academy, a school in western Massachusetts I'd never heard of before but that I liked a lot when Mom took me up there.

"You know, Bumppo, we've been talking here now for maybe a year, off and on. I tink I know you. Right now, you are down. You feel like you're not smart. Belief me, your brain iss okay, it's just not tinking quite right. It's not understanding dat vhat dis man – so-called 'teacher'—did to you vas a terrible ting. You must not let yourself believe—not for a minute—vhat dis Leonard guy did vas right. De truth iss dat dis vorld iss full of good people and some not-so-good people, you know dat. You are a good guy and dis Leonard is not a good guy. Maybe you know vhat happened to me during de Var?"

"Yes, Mrs. Kertess told me a little about it. She said you never talked about it because you don't want to even think about it."

"True, but it's vith me every day—every minute, in fact. It's vith me every time I tink, maybe, I stay at de office and vork some more. 'Don't do it—go home,' I hear a voice say inside my head. 'Read a good book. Talk to a young person like Bumppo and find out vhat's going on vith him. Enjoy vhat's left of your life,' it says. Vhen I get down—and, belief me, it happens—de voice says: 'So you feel sorry for yourself. Boo hoo. You got a bad deal. So vhat? Are you alife now or are you going to mope around about vhat happened to you? It's over. It's gone. Forget it.' And vhat's it's really telling me is dat I haff choices every day to do tings I vant to do or to do tings just because somebody else vants me to do dem. I haff a choice to close myself off from de world and mope or open myself up to all de good tings I missed before. I haff a choice to get mad about vhat happened to me or I can forget about it. You haff the same kind of choice, Bumppo. Vhat kind of a man you are going to be, you must decide. No one does dat for you. If dis Leonard guy iss going to get you, you vill be making a choice to let him get you. Or, you can forget it."

"I just can't understand why he wanted to hurt me so much." My voice sounded strangled. "I want to know!"

"You tink too much. Vhat does it matter, why? Maybe he's a sadist. Maybe it was his vay of pulling your fingernails out one by one."

"I did feel like I was being tortured. It was pretty awful every time I went to his class."

"No vonder."

"I also got to thinking that maybe I deserved those crummy grades. I couldn't believe he'd just make them up."

"You belief that now?"

"I don't know. Maybe."

"Tell you vhat. You go to dis Villiston Academy. You vill try to do good, I'm sure of dat. And you vill do good, I'm also sure of dat. Maybe you don't tink so yet, but I know you. You come to see me at Thanksgifing or Christmas or sometime, and I bet you vill believe it den, okay?"

I said okay, I'd come and see him at Thanksgiving.

"And, I vant you to remember something. You know I sometimes read philosophers. A Roman who lived 2000 years ago said someting I remember because it meant so much to me. It helped me and maybe it vill help you. It goes someting like this in English: 'fire iss de test of gold; adversity iss de test of strong men.' Remember: this is your test, Bumppo, and I know you vill pass it because you are strong."

Chapter Seven

WILLISTON WAS A lot smaller than Exeter, a bit closer to home, and not nearly as well-heeled. Its humble origins lay in the charity of Samuel Williston, a nineteenth century button manufacturer who left a sliver of his fortune to a boy's school he'd started to impress his Christian ideals on the children of the clerks and other white-collar workers at his factory. Long after he'd met his Maker, the school was opened to boys from the neighboring western Massachusetts towns, and even, like me, from beyond New England.

The Schoolhouse, Williston's main building, was an old brick button factory converted to its present use when the textile industry in New England withered and moved South for cheaper labor. The descendants of the Founder eventually closed the button factory, converted some of the decaying buildings into classrooms, and merged the tiny school the Founder had started into what was now Williston Academy. Apparently, they didn't have much use for books. Williston's miniscule library was so small and poorly stocked, to do any serious reading—and I was reading a lot—I had to go to the modest, but still larger, town library and apply for a public library card. Amazed, the librarian said that I was the first Williston student she could remember doing that.

The dorm I was assigned to was a recently, and cheaply built, long, two-story rectangle with a flat roof. Inside, the unplastered concrete block walls were painted that unique and sickly green color I'd seen only in hospitals and my public school in Dobbs Ferry. Where does it come from? The brown linoleum tile floors were exactly the same temperature as outdoors, especially in the winter. My hollow wooden door wasn't hung properly and couldn't be shut completely. My bed was of the steel military cot variety with wire mesh springs for which the school supplied two thin gray blankets and a lumpy, under-feathered pillow. I brought sheets from home which I had to launder myself occasionally when they became the same gray as the blankets and, perhaps, life-threatening. My closet was a tiny corner of my room blocked off by accordion-style, plastic folding doors which didn't work.

The building hadn't even been named when I first moved in, obviously because no thinking person wanted his good name associated with it. "Where do you live, son?" Dad asked me when I called home during the first week of school.

"In a dorm," I said.

"What's its name," he asked

"I don't think it has a name," I replied.

"Oh," he said after a long moment. I don't think he was surprised.

A couple of weeks after that conversation, the Headmaster—
whom I called Mr. Stevens, not "Phil"—referred to it as
"Memorial Hall," so I guess it did have a name all along. Mr.
Stevens didn't say what it was named in memory of or why it had
been left totally unfinished and almost unlivable. I guessed the
school didn't have much money.

When I saw my room in what I thought was a nameless dorm
for the first time, my melancholy thoughts of the summer before
returned: I had been sentenced to do time here. I was guilty of
something and deserved to be punished. When I met Jody, my
new roommate, with whom I would be forced to spend the next
year, I became very suspicious that Williston was really a reform
school or some kind of penal institution masquerading as a normal school and this silent, glowering hulk had been made my cell
mate for added punishment. He never said anything but would
sit in his wooden chair with both arms on his desk enveloping a
textbook. He'd stare vacantly at the book, toying with a brown
metal gooseneck lamp hour after hour to pass the time. And, the
bells confirmed my suspicions—those ever-present clanging, in-
stitutional bells: loud bells, louder than fire alarms, jolting me
awake at seven o'clock, telling me when to eat, when to begin a
class and when a class ended. Bells for studying, bells to stop
studying, and bells for lights out. Bells I'll probably hear in my
memory for the rest of my life. Why hadn't I seen these things
before I decided to come here?

Worse, I was now surrounded by "nubbies"—my word for boys
who wore jackets with little speckles of colored thread. Williston

was overrun by nubbies. They were everywhere! All of a sudden, I was the outsider. Would the wheel turn completely against me? Would they make me the victim of their cruel, unfair and un-thinking bigotry? How suspicious I was of them, sure that they were every bit as intolerant of people like me as people like me at Exeter were of them. I was afraid of them. After all, many of them were only slightly de-greased versions of the high school hoods, with their leather jackets, slick DAs and chopped and channeled hot rods, who used to thunder through the streets of Hastings, Dobbs Ferry, Irvington and Tarrytown, the little sub-urban Westchester towns along the Hudson River near Ardsley, looking for guys like me to punch out just for fun. I was afraid of the hostility I believed they must have for me, a preppy who represented a group they must deeply hate for the money and advantages they thought we had.

How wrong I was. Sure, they were suspicious of me, probably because they thought I must feel superior to them, that I'd laugh at them and try to put them down, but I soon found out that there was no group ethic that told them they should hate me, not like at Exeter. After we got used to each other's strangeness, they accepted me—even if I didn't have a ready label like Polack, Wop, Hebe, Harp, or Spic, words that would have been fatal for me to utter, but were okay for the kids themselves to use as a form of ethnic self-identity. Some even felt sorry for me that I wasn't any of those things. I was what was left over—the "other" at the end of the ethnic questionnaire. But, I got over it and be-gan to see the nubbies' strong points.

In one of my first English classes at Williston, my teach-er, Charles Rouse, whom everyone called "Chuck," read Carl

Sandburg's poem "Chicago:" He intoned the words in a deep rumbling basso:

> *Hog Butcher for the World,*
> *Tool Maker, Stacker of Wheat...*
> *Stormy, husky, brawling,*
> *City of the Big Shoulders.*

Those muscular words got me to daydreaming about the nubbies around me and how my own ancestry was full of really boring New England farmers and preachers. But, the nubbies! They came from wonderful stock: honest, God-fearing workers-with-their-hands, tillers-of-the-soil, men-against-the-sea. Drunk with Sandburg, I could see ovens full of baking bread; hellish furnace fires of foundries fed by strong arms and muscled backs glistening with sweat; solitary farmers trudging doggedly behind horse-drawn plows long after sunset; wave-washed, wind-beaten fishermen straining to haul in their nets heavy with fish from the ice-cold sea; men and women living out their entire lives in giant factories full of crashing, thundering machines, weaving, spinning, stamping, punching, printing; blackened faces and white eyes of miners reaching the surface in the evening of another day, another day, and another. They came to this country stormy, husky, brawling, Men with Big Shoulders.

My daydream ended when I suddenly heard laughter all around me. Startled, I looked up and saw that the rest of the class was looking at me and laughing. Why? I was confused. Then, Mr. Rouse asked me, I guess for the third or fourth time, if I wanted to join the class or take a nap.

My best friends that year were a boy from nearby Shelburne Falls, Bruce Eldridge, and, a passionately ambitious and horny Jew from Washington, D.C., Steve David. Bruce owned only a single jacket (dark brown with orange nubbies), no suit, had never traveled farther than Springfield, Massachusetts, and saw no need to. Steve, whose brilliance had barely survived his rotten public school education, prided himself on being a "real sharp" dresser. His entire wardrobe consisted of a white jacket with black nubbies, a black jacket with white nubbies, an enormous black and yellow floral tie he wore with both jackets, one pair of black pants and a pair of strange, crepe-soled shoes he called his "brothel-creepers."

The bells at Williston rang at 7 a.m. for wake-up; 7:30 for breakfast; 8:15 for the first class period, and so on all day long, every day, except Sunday. The entire cycle of the ordinary day was completely different from the unstructured life I was used to at Exeter. Here, there were mandatory study halls—unheard of at Exeter; required attendance at meals—unenforceable at Exeter; assigned seats for every meal at various master's tables on a rotating basis with attendance taken; mandatory chapels; and required sports which I couldn't avoid even if I'd tried—but I didn't try. In fact, from my first day there, I was determined to learn the ropes, the culture of this place, as quickly as possible and do everything "their" way, like it or not. I knew that choosing the rules I'd obey was one of my problems at Exeter. If I hadn't broken the rule against smoking, I probably would never have gotten to know Black Sam and the other bridge addicts; if I hadn't been playing bridge in the Wentworth buttroom, I might still be at Exeter getting fantastic grades from Chilson

Leonard. Or would I? I often brooded about what I did wrong at Exeter during my first months at Williston, kicking myself for being so dumb that I was now in a strange ethnic melting pot. If I'd been really smart, I'd still be playing bridge in my beloved smoke-filled buttrooms, occasionally spending weekends getting sloshed on beer at Harvard with Bob, and otherwise easing by with as little work as possible. "Easing by" had also meant, of course, easing into Harvard, where I had always assumed, without question, I would go, and where I truly believed that the card games and comradeship of the basement buttrooms would simply continue in new and better accommodations, free of even the minimal constraints we recognized at Exeter. Now, however, Harvard was unthinkable for me—literally unthinkable. I knew I'd never go there and, in fact, had the miserable feeling that I would not go to college anywhere, nowhere at all; time would simply stop at graduation. I had thrown my entire life away.

A small speck of hope clung to me like lint I couldn't brush off. My little inner voice kept telling me that, although it was probably dumb to think I had a real chance of getting back on course, if I did have any chance at all to salvage a reasonable life, this time I'd better do it right and not screw it up by bucking the rules of this place. So I lived by those damned bells, was never late or missed anything, and slowly began to participate in activities—like the school newspaper, *The Willistonian*, and the glee club. And, I stopped smoking. I didn't stop following Gil Hodges and the Dodgers. They won their first World Series that fall beating the Yankees in seven games, which was amazing. Hodges didn't have as good a year as the year before when he'd had 42 homers—second best that year in the Major Leagues—

but he'd had a pretty good year and got a key hit that won one of the Series games. I still followed him every day of the season just as I'd done every summer before. I'd never forget listening to the radio on August 31, 1950 when Hodges hit four homers in one game. Only a few players, including Lou Gehrig, had ever done that, and Hodges also hit a single in that game.

Slowly, but very definitely, things began changing for the better. No one, students or faculty, seemed to know anything about my dark past, or care. No one knew that I'd gotten some of the worst grades in history and flunked English II at Exeter. So, I was a clean slate and, as I began to contribute to the life of the school, it began to reward me, to nourish me as a fresh bud on the stem. I liked that. I definitely liked feeling that I was a fresh bud.

OFTEN, I WISHED that I could draw more than the intricate doodles that decorated my notebooks. I wished I had the talent to paint the glorious hills blazing with the fiery reds and oranges of the turning leaves in the morning autumn sun as they emerged from the shadow of Mt. Tom, which loomed over the campus to the east. Like the reproduction of a wonderful Thomas Cole painting I saw in the Easthampton Public Library, my painting would mysteriously capture the presence of a divinity in ancient trees and rocks—not a god who had simply designed this world as a wonderfully intricate mechanism and wound it up and then abandoned it, leaving it to run untended and uncared for through countless seasons and millennia until it would simply stop one day. No, the divinity in my painting would be visible—in the leaves, absorbed, like the squirrels, with the important business of ensuring life in the coming colder days and as a beautiful bird soaring high over the rocks and trees on the slopes of Mt. Tom, watching over His creation. Mr. Stevens, whom I thought of as "Phil" when he wasn't around, had told me early in the year that "It is good for a boy to grow up in the shadow of a mountain." I gagged when I heard it, but after I'd heard Phil say it to others and after I'd looked around me and become aware of the serene beauty of the hills that surrounded me at Williston as I became familiar with my new school's buildings and rhythms that fall, it actually began to make some sense.

I knew I needed that serenity to help me recover from the poison fog at home. Here, there was no fog. The air was fresh and sweet. The silence of the hills was the peace of contentment, not the brittle silence of angry people not talking. That peace also helped me face the important business of recuperating from what I now thought of as a major operation—my extraction, like a diseased tooth, from Exeter. No matter how pointless Dad thought my life had become, I had to try to change it. I had to try; it was my life, not his. I looked around at the hills a lot and got to know the habits of a red-tailed hawk as it soared in circles over the woods beyond the football field. I watched that hawk a lot. When it spotted prey, it would fold its wings and plummet to earth like a stone. It would come out of free-fall at the last possible moment before crashing to grab the chipmunk or whatever in its talons and fly off to its nest. I wanted to be like that hawk, and learn how to catch what I was going after, instead of crashing. I'd already done that.

I didn't have any plan to snatch victory in my talons, but I did know that, if I had any hope at all of academic resurrection,

I had to begin with making a good impression on every single one of my teachers right from the start. How in the world to do that was a real problem, mostly because I suspected that all the teachers already knew too much about me—maybe some of them even knew Chilson Leonard. If they did know Mr. Leonard, or about what had happened at Exeter, I was sure they already thought I would never amount to much, or else why would I be at Williston?

I also knew that I couldn't hide in class. I couldn't do what I desperately wanted to do—avoid any contact with teachers and stay anonymous. I had no experience with raising my hand and speaking in any class, much less standing out at anything, except in Mr. Leonard's class before the nightmare began. Being excellent at anything—except, maybe, bridge—was not something I'd wanted to be, at least until now. Now, I doubted that I could ever really do well at anything. I also doubted, deeply, my ability to predict very well how adults would behave, and that led me to think that, without reliable radar, I should do my best to avoid the enemy entirely whenever possible. But, the rules were different now. Here, I needed adults. I had to impress my teachers. Try flying without radar and see what happens.

While some of my new friends at Williston had also been bounced from other schools and had to make re-entry adjustments as I did, several pretended to be cynical about everything—the bells, the rules, the other guys, their own families. Other students—in fact, most of them—had gone to public schools and thought that getting into Williston the best thing that ever happened to them. They were proud of their roots and families in a way that made me envy them. I knew it meant a lot to them that their brothers and sisters and uncles and aunts at home, and their grandparents, maybe in the old country, were all pulling for them. I assumed Bob was pulling for me but he didn't ask and I didn't tell him. While I knew Mom was pulling for me, I don't think I crossed Dad's mind, except maybe when he had to pay my tuition. I was sure that he wondered why he was doing that. The pride those other kids had made them pretty serious about what they were doing at Williston. They weren't there to grease into some Ivy League college because they didn't know what else to do with their lives.

It occurred to me then for the first time that I felt no responsibility to anyone, especially myself, to become educated, and the only obligation I'd ever felt was not to screw up in a way that would embarrass my parents, and I'd already done that. So, I had to try something new. Williston helped me do that. Every one of my teachers assumed that most of us were there to do the best we could, and that all of us needed help and support, some more than others, but everyone sometimes, and there was no shame in asking. We were there to learn, not to waste time, and anything that helped was okay.

I certainly needed support when I arrived, and it didn't take long to find it. On the second day of school, Chuck Rouse, my English III teacher—Williston had given me credit for English II despite Leonard's 59—took me aside after he'd graded and returned our first written efforts for him. My paper came back without any grade. Oh my God, I thought as my classmates left the room with their grades. I was frantically searched on the front and back of each page hoping the mark was buried somewhere I'd missed. Mr. Rouse was standing by my desk, watching me. He said he didn't want to grade my paper, that any grade he gave would imply that it fell somewhere within the range he was used to, but my paper didn't fit into that spectrum at all. I became woozy with horror—the one talent I once believed in had again betrayed me, as it had at Exeter. Damn! Chilson Leonard was right! How could I have written something so off the wall that he couldn't even give me a grade? How come I didn't even fit into his frigging spectrum, whatever that meant? I was so upset I even forgot what I'd written about. Then I heard him saying that, if I was willing, he'd like to work with me, perhaps on some special projects we could come up with, like a literary supplement for the school newspaper. He'd always wanted to do a supplement. Was I interested?

"Sure," I stammered, "but my paper—was it okay?"

"Yes, indeed," he'd said, "it was better than okay. You've got something special, Nathaniel. Don't worry about grades. Write for yourself. Listen to what you write. Like music, there is a lilt and rhythm to good writing. You've got an ear for that, and that's what we should work on, letting you hear the music of what you read and write."

I wrote a lot for Mr. Rouse, infected by his enthusiasm. He was like a chipmunk with his quick, twitchy movements and buck teeth, always smiling, always moving, looking around for something, walking around, sitting down, standing up, turning around, scratching his bald head, playing with his glasses, tweaking his bow tie, talking all the time, asking questions, not always waiting for the answers. The more I worked with him, I feared him less and less. In fact, I began to think that even though he'd read a lot, he wasn't so smart. After all, he liked my stuff! I began to argue with him about the essays he gave us to read by critics on the poems and books we'd finished. Some were just plain hogwash, pompous and bloated and dumb. Mostly, it was the symbolism these critics found that turned me off and nearly ruined some pretty good books for me. Sometimes, Mr. Rouse bought it, and sometimes he didn't.

Once, when we were discussing a long critical essay in the front of the students' edition of *The Adventures of Huckleberry Finn* we'd been given, Mr. Rouse asked me what I thought of it. I'd thought it was a pretentious piece of garbage, as far as I could see, but didn't want to say it that way.

"Not too much really," I said.

"Well I don't understand that. I thought it was pretty insightful—even profound. What was wrong with it, in your exalted view, Professor Bickford?"

"I thought all that malarkey about Huck and Jim being a 'community of saints' searching for God together, like the entire Family of Man, on the River of Life was just too much! It almost ruined the book for me, thinking that, maybe, Mark Twain really meant all that stuff, which I don't think he did. To be frank, it almost made me puke."

"It almost made you puke? PUKE!"—Mr. Rouse looked a little upset; his face was getting red. "Do you know who wrote that piece?"

"Uh…a man named Trilling, I think."

"It was Lionel Trilling—a distinguished man of letters and thought by many to be one of the greatest living critics of American fiction!" His voice was a bit edgy.

"Oh, I didn't know that, but I still don't think he's right. I don't think Mark Twain would have wanted anyone to read *Huck Finn* that way. It's not like *Moby-Dick* where you know that Ahab and the white whale are symbols—Good and Evil, Man's Search for God, or something like that. But, not Huck and Black Jim. No way! So, I still think Professor what's-his-name is full of BS," I said defensively scrunching down in my seat.

"Do you think it is even remotely possible," Mr. Rouse began, his voice rising and some redness creeping into his cheeks, "that a man who has reached the height of his considerable powers and earned the respect of his colleagues in every institution of higher learning from Coast to Coast—a man who has been asked, alone among hundreds of others, to write the introduction to this Student Edition by one of the finest academic publishers in the country, knowing that tens of thousands of students will read it—do you really think for one second that such a man could be simply 'full of BS,' as you put it?" Mr. Rouse's voice ended in a grand crescendo and reverberated throughout the entire room before I could answer.

"Well…yes…Sir," I said, very meekly, almost with a question mark.

"Well, so do I," he said, the fierce look on his face replaced with a big grin.

What a sight he was with that big grin—big beaver teeth, striped bow tie and his shiny bald head fringed with white hair that looked like feathers. He liked zinging it to me, sticking his chin out as if he was begging me to punch it. Somehow I knew that he wasn't looking for an excuse to jump all over me. Instead, he wanted to get me to take my best shot. This surely wasn't the kind of behavior I was used to or expected from adults who, mostly, told me what I should think. Because of that, I didn't believe that my opinions mattered much. After all, even my friends came to believe that what I had to say was worthless in Mr. Leonard's English class. So, why should this new teacher really want to hear what I had to say? He kept poking at me and, before I was completely aware of it, I wasn't hiding in a back seat anymore, staring at the floor, trying to avoid him. No, sir! I was pumped up, sometimes going mano-a-mano with him, sometimes even winning. Maybe, he let me win. I wasn't sure about that.

I was pretty sure that if I went mano-a-mano with Archibald Hepworth, I'd lose every time. What he expected of us was unbelievable. He taught American History and was the Varsity Tennis coach, the two arenas where I saw him, and they were definitely arenas—like boxing rings. Success, in Mr. Hepworth's terms, was measured by the degree to which you fell short of his expectations; if you were still standing, that was good. He punched and probed like Mr. Rouse, but, if he didn't get an answer he wanted, or someone said something outlandish, he'd rifle a felt blackboard eraser at the head of the offender with the speed and accuracy of Warren Spahn.

Mr. Hepworth looked a lot like Chilson Leonard. He was a bull of a man like Mr. Leonard, but where Mr. Leonard was quiet and a little sneaky, Hepworth was vigorous and powerful and explosive in everything he did and said. If he came into a room, everyone would stop and wait for him to take over. He was a force like a hurricane that moved everything. He oozed strength and authority. So, I studied a lot and almost looked forward to his next assault so that I could give him some nugget I hoped the others would miss. As I used to do with Chilson Leonard, I tried to play Mr. Hepworth's game, once I knew the rules, and that took a lot of work, believe me. You'd have to know the facts, for sure, but also be able to recall them instantly as Mr. Hepworth almost danced through his class whirling, pointing, demanding answers, flinching with pain when the answer was wrong or took too long, and hurling that eraser if the answer was really dumb. He got beyond historical facts to see what was really going on during things like the Constitutional Conventions, the Civil War and the New Deal. He made us feel Teddy Roosevelt's energy and vigor—in fact, we all thought that maybe Teddy had been reincarnated as Hepworth—but we also felt we got to know some others personally. What a surprise to discover that George Washington was truly heroic and admirable and not the plastic saint who couldn't lie; or, that marvelously inventive Ben Franklin was also conniving and horny, seducing older women when he was in Paris because they were "more grateful;" or, that brilliant, versatile Jefferson could write the Declaration of Independence and also design graceful buildings; or, that melancholy, saintly Lincoln, was surprisingly despised by so many in his time; and, that patrician FDR was such an unlikely revolutionary. They all came alive and I was sure they would stay with me forever.

Many of my new classmates didn't realize that there was fun in this, and they cowered, hoping desperately they wouldn't be called on. As for me, who'd developed avoiding classroom discussions of any kind into an art at Exeter, I spent the year in nervous anxiety, and even excitement, on the edge of my seat, hoping I'd found every nugget he could possibly ask for and never sure. I got better at it as time went by, but Mr. Hepworth didn't reward routine accomplishment—he expected that. So, over-prepared and hyped up as I was, still I rarely earned the only reward Mr. Hepworth ever gave: he'd freeze in his tracks, peer over his half-glasses with a surprised twinkle in his eye and bellow: "Well done, young man!"

On the tennis court, Hepworth was an odd sight—a blue school athletic jacket half zipped up the huge barrel chest that was perched on thick stumpy legs in skimpy blue gym shorts. He paced around furiously barking orders. In fact, when we heard he'd been a Navy officer during the war, we thought he was trying to order us around just the same way he must have terrorized the crew of the destroyer he'd commanded in the Pacific. His expectations for us were huge, but the level of our athletic abilities almost always fell far short of his Olympian hopes. So, being around us and having to deal with our shortcomings produced an irrepressible pressure in him to release his frustrations somehow, without resorting to the usual obscenities forbidden to him as our moral superior. So, he created his own: a guttural Germanic cough that sounded something like "schrecklech," which he spat out when displeased. Its frequency was a good measure of how we were doing and we heard it a lot. We speculated on its meaning since he wouldn't tell us. I thought, maybe, it was made-up. I used to catch myself saying it sometimes until I realized that, whatever it meant in German, it was Hepworth's word, perfectly consistent with his character, but not mine. I could not be Hepworth, but I could learn from him.

McCall Maxwell was altogether different. If Hepworth was Teddy Roosevelt to me, Mr. Maxwell was Adlai Stevenson— urbane and sophisticated and worldly-wise. He was always impeccable in his button-down striped shirts, gray flannels, well-tailored blue blazers with custom-made gold buttons and penny loafers—all from Brooks Brothers—somehow living comfortably in this land of nubbies and Buster Browns.

Mr. Maxwell taught French, which I didn't take but sometimes wished I had since I heard that he spent as much time in his class talking about wines and how great France is as he did on the language. He used French phrases all the time in regular conversations, making him sound smart and sophisticated. If the rules said you have to do something, he always said it is *de rigeur* or if something had to be done right away it was always *tout de suite*. If he agreed with something someone else said, he'd reply *bien sur* or *mais oui*.

Even though I wasn't in Mr. Maxwell's French class, I saw him almost every day, especially after I signed up for *The Willistonian*, the school newspaper. Mr. Maxwell was its faculty advisor and was always around when we edited the paper and pasted up the galleys. I wrote an overdone, but accurate, attack on the shoddy construction of my nameless cinder-block dorm. My article—to be accompanied by a photograph of my broken plastic folding door drooping sadly in the corner of my room—blamed "the Administration"—meaning, of course, him, since he was Assistant Headmaster, in charge of things with Phil Stevens away a lot concentrating on raising money and meeting with trustees and others off the campus. Mr. Maxwell coaxed me into killing that story myself without even raising his voice. I don't know how he did it. Was he smooth!

Why he took to me, I didn't know and I was pretty sure it wouldn't last when he got to know me. Maybe, he liked me because I was more preppy than a lot of the other kids there, other than the other prep school rejects like me, that is. Didn't he know I wasn't so smart? In his official Assistant Headmaster role, he could easily have seen my transcript which would have shown that I flunked English II.

Mr. Maxwell seemed to like me right away. He asked me to have coffee with him a lot, sometimes in his apartment on the top floor of Ford Hall, the senior dorm which, without him, was forbidden territory to juniors like me. His door was always open and I began to notice as I went there more often that the same bunch of seniors seemed to hang out there. I also saw that they treated him with an easy familiarity, calling him "Mac" and bantering with him. Fooling around with a teacher like that was something I understood, but since it hadn't worked out too well for me with Chilson Leonard, I was pretty formal with Mr. Maxwell even though I tried not to be. I hardly ever called him "Mac"—at least at school. It didn't seem right to be that friendly with a teacher.

Mr. Maxwell knew the theater district around Broadway inside out and loved nothing better than a night on the town in New York City—drinks at the Mayan Room in Rockefeller Center where his friend Marian McPartland played at the chic piano bar, then dinner at some out-of-the-way French bistro he had a knack for discovering, and, finally, seeing the latest play on Broadway. I had two outings in the City like that with him during my first Christmas vacation from Williston, just me and him. On the second of these, just before New Year's, he took me to see *Cat on a Hot Tin Roof,* which I liked a lot, for my sixteenth birthday. "Mac," because he insisted that I call him that when we weren't at school, wanted to talk about Ben Gazzara's role as the injured and troubled athlete Brick, but I was more interested in Burl Ives, who was wonderfully disgusting as Big Daddy, and much more interested in Barbara Bel Geddes as sexy Maggie—the "Cat"—who really got to me. I couldn't understand why Brick didn't want to spend his entire life in the sack with Maggie, let alone not go to bed with her at all. Mac seemed to understand that, but couldn't explain it to me.

These were exciting and slightly dangerous adventures, since cocktails were not a part of my normal routine and I didn't drink at all at home, at least as far as my parents knew. Most of all, they meant to me that, despite Mr. Leonard and Exeter, maybe I was acceptable company for intelligent, civilized people after all, or at least one intelligent, civilized person. That was a pretty good beginning.

BRUCE ELDRIDGE, A STUDENT from nearby Shelburne Falls, was a whiz with anything electronic and had no use for books. He thought reading anything other than schematic drawings of electrical circuits, was a huge waste of time. I hung out a lot with him and horny Steve David, Joe Hine, a laid-back preppie from Long Island who dreamed of his red TR3 which he wasn't allowed to have at school, Art Pellman, a very good guy with a bad Brooklyn accent, and, Corby Finney, deeply pessimistic and sarcastic, who reminded me a lot of snide, smirking Bob Downey at Exeter. (I heard that fall that Downey had died when he drove a car off the road into a tree. I wondered if he'd done it on purpose.) Joe Hine was a Brooks Brothers and Harris Tweed type; Finney was never without his blue blazer, a shirt with tabs on the collar and a rep tie. Art Pellman was a shapeless sack; in the winter, he looked like a bear in his too-large brown overcoat and woolen hat with earmuffs that tied under his chin, head scrunched down so that he had no neck, just eyes squinting painfully through thick, horn-rimmed glasses as he blundered around school in the snow.

Bruce, Steve and Art wouldn't have gotten past the interview stage at Exeter, but probably would never have applied. Joe was so laid back that he wouldn't have gone to an interview in the first place and Finney would have killed his chances with an acid comment about how crummy an experience he was bound to have there. Even if all of them had gotten into Exeter, they wouldn't have met each other, much less become friends. Here at Williston, it was different. There were no untouchables. What anybody wore didn't matter.

Our meeting place was DeBarbieri's Luncheonette and Soda Shoppe which had a long counter with stools, a few booths, a jukebox with a hundred songs and Helen, the wife of Frank, the owner, who we never saw. It was a bit of an armpit, but we headed there whenever we could and played the juke box—Dean Martin oozing "Memories Are Made of This" was big that year—and shot the breeze with Helen who was always in the middle of some huge domestic crisis with her brutal drunk of a husband or Boris, her hulking, truly scary Bulgarian lover, who made the burgers and never said a word. Helen, old at thirty something, had had a daughter when she was in high school and dropped out. She envied us. She thought we all were very smart and would make something of ourselves, unlike herself. I wasn't so sure. I wanted to tell her that we probably wouldn't amount to anything either, to make her feel better, but I didn't.

George Black, the captain of the tennis team and by then a good friend even though he was a class ahead of me, asked me to go to Delray Beach, Florida, for spring vacation with him; we'd stay with his parents and be able to play a lot of tennis as well as explore the delights of Florida. I would need some money for a train ticket and other expenses down there, which meant I'd have to ask my parents for it.

Hoping to avoid asking Dad for the money for Florida, I asked Mom. She said I couldn't go because it would cost a lot for my food and the train tickets down and back and other things, and she didn't have it. So, since I really wanted to go, I asked Dad when he came home from work that night. "Sure," he said. "No problem," and didn't even ask how much I needed. When I told Mom that Dad had said I could go, she looked a little testy and said fine, go ahead, enjoy yourself. She didn't seem too happy about it. I wanted to understand all this better, so I asked her why could Dad just say okay, but she didn't think we had the money? She seemed a bit irritated and said I should ask Dad that same question, so I did.

I found Dad sitting at a table at the end of the living room. He had a yellow pad and a lot of papers spread out all over the table, and was reading stuff that looked like work from his office and making notes on the pad with a pencil. When I saw that he was concentrating, I thought maybe I should wait. Then I thought if I waited I wouldn't ask him at all, so I plunged in.

"Dad, sorry to interrupt, but I've got something I want to ask you about."

He looked up and put down the pencil. "What's on your mind?"

"Well, before I asked you if I could go Florida with George Black and his parents, I asked Mom if I could go and she said no because we don't have the money for the train tickets and everything else. Then, when you came home and I asked you, you said fine, I could go. And that's great. I really want to go. But, how come Mom said I couldn't go? I mean she knows that we either have the money or we don't, doesn't she?"

Dad looked tense. He stood up and began walking around in circles in the middle of the living room stroking the back of his head with a pained look on his face. He slumped down on the big couch. It was a couple of minutes before he said anything. Then he glared at me as if he was about to punish me for doing something really bad. "That's all you three care about, isn't it?" he asked in a normal voice like he was asking if I'd let the dogs out in the backyard recently. I wasn't about to answer. He stood up and almost shouted at me: "I mean how much you can get out of me and how much I'm worth—that's all you care about! Well, you can tell your mother and your brother that I'm worth a lot more dead than alive. I've got a lot of life insurance, so if I die, you'll all be happy."

I never did get an answer to my question, but I did find out why Mom never asked him about money very much, except occasionally when she needed a raise. I decided I would never ask him about his money again.

IN MAY, TO give us a break from studying for our final exams, Mac took me and Tom Mickle, a quiet, preppy blond kid who grew up in Brazil, I think, and now lived in Greenwich, to a concert by Eugene Ormandy and the Philadelphia Orchestra at

the Academy Playhouse near Smith College in Northampton. I
didn't really want to go. I didn't know Tom very well, except
as one of the guys who hung around Mr. Maxwell, and I could
think of a lot of things I'd rather do. But, since I didn't feel like
studying and I'd never been to a concert before and Mr. Maxwell
made it clear that he'd be disappointed if I didn't go, I went—
all dressed up in my one white button-down shirt, rep tie, blue
blazer and gray flannel pants, just like Mac and Tom.

I trudged to my seat between Tom and Mr. Maxwell in the
first row on one side of the balcony and noticed immediately
that I could lean over the rail and look right down into the violin
section of the orchestra. That was good because, without an interesting diversion, I was afraid I might fall asleep before the end
and roll out of my seat over the edge of the balcony. I vowed that
I would never again be cajoled into going to another concert.

The lights went down and Eugene Ormandy, who Mr. Maxwell
said was a very great conductor, held his arms out with a baton
in his right hand poised like a sword. Everything was totally
quiet for a long moment and then the sword flashed down and
the music began. It was a short piece by Ralph Vaughn Williams
called "Fantasia on a Theme by Thomas Tallis." I knew the
theme immediately because it was the same tune as a hymn I'd
sung in church but the composer had transformed it and made
it mystical and magical. I began to "see" the color red as the orchestra played the tune I knew, not bright red but darker, maybe
the color of blood, with oranges and browns swirling around
the red. I could still see the orchestra and everything else, but
it was like looking through a colored filter. Then—pow—the
violins soared high and the cellos and basses zoomed low, white

light exploded around me and, suddenly, I was physically inside the music. I could still see the auditorium and the orchestra and everything else; what I was "seeing" didn't blot out anything but simply appeared in front of everything so that I was looking through the colors that were changing and pulsating with the music. I knew that it had something to do with the music because it was as if I was "seeing" the music itself in another form. As the sound changed, the colors changed.

I was wrecked. I snuck out the side and went to the bathroom, worried about what had just happened to me and whether I was losing my marbles. I stayed outside for the entire next piece, which was something by Mozart but, even outside, when I shut my eyes listening to it, I "saw" wonderful white light bouncing off the crystal chandeliers in the foyer.

I met Tom and Mac as they came out at the intermission. Mr. Maxwell asked me if everything was okay and how I liked the first part. I said I was fine and that the music was really great, which is what I would have said even if I'd hated it, which I didn't, but I also didn't know what to say had happened to me. Maybe it happened to everyone? I didn't think so.

The second half of the concert was Tchaikovsky's Sixth Symphony, called "Pathetique," and I listened. Again, I found myself seeing things. This time I was surrounded by something that felt warm and I "saw" astonishing colors—flashing reds and blues as the violins soared, yellow lightning when the cymbals clashed and muddy browns when the timpani rolled. It was amazing. I just knew that the music had colors that I could feel without actually seeing them like a mirage or a hallucination. At the end of the second movement, the concert hall was full of an iridescent blue. In the third movement, I "saw" arcs of light. The last movement was full of black clouds that overcame any light and color until everything was black. That was the way it ended. All black.

When it was over, I was wet and exhausted, as if I'd just played five close sets of tennis with a really good player and gotten beaten. What in the world had happened? Mac said something like: "You looked like you were really into it, Bumppo. Isn't 'Pathetique' a wonderful piece, full of color and emotion?" He used the word "color," and I couldn't have agreed with him more. "Yeah," I said. "It really did have amazing colors." For a second, Mr. Maxwell looked at me strangely and then we were leaving the hall with the rest of the crowd. When we got in Mac's car for the ride back to Williston, he asked me what I meant by my comment about the music having "amazing colors"—he emphasized the plural. So, I told him what had happened to me and what I'd "seen." He said he'd have to think about it. I wasn't sure he believed me. About a week later, he mentioned the concert again and said that he thought I had a special gift and that he'd always suspected extraordinary things of me. While all that made me a little uncomfortable, I have to say that I liked it. In fact, a lot of the personal things he'd said about me made me uncomfortable, but it was a lot better to have a teacher—and a powerful one at that—saying good things about me than trying to ruin my life.

Years later, I heard that "seeing" colors when listening to music isn't all that unusual. Some people "see" numbers as having colors—as Vladimir Nabokov and his mother did, as he described in his memoir *Speak, Memory*—and some people hear sounds with numbers. People who have multiple sensory experiences such as these are known as "synaesthetes." Of course, it would be years before I learned anything about the condition, years during which it faded considerably, but not entirely. It still occurs when I concentrate on music, particularly symphonic and some choral music.

TOWARD THE END of the Spring Term, Mac somehow talked me into running for next year's Student Council. I never would have considered it for a minute because I was terrified of public speaking—I just froze solid—and "public" meant even two adults. He said winning the election would look great on my college applications and would bring some highly desirable senior-year perks, like staying up later, for example. I just didn't know if I could handle the public speaking part, but Mac persuaded me to take the risk. He made it personal, as if I didn't run, I'd be disappointing him, and I couldn't do that.

IN EARLY JUNE, Mom and Dad drove up to Williston to take me home after the graduation exercises. We sat on metal folding chairs in the gym full of the families and friends of the graduating seniors, and watched as each senior marched single-file up to the specially-built platform draped with the school's banner and covered with flowers in Williston's colors of blue and gold, and sat down. I was a part of it all. I wasn't a bystander watching someone else's parade, like I was at Bob's graduation. There was my friend George Black, captain of the varsity tennis team—I'd played third singles and second doubles with him, had a winning year and would be captain myself next year; wise-cracking Arie Kopelman, impersonator of faculty and extraordinary wit; Frank

Knight, with a biting sense of humor as good as Kopelman's—
each of them the equal of any stand-up comic. I liked them all. I
liked this school. I belonged.

Headmaster Phillips Stevens looked like a splendid magician
in the black robe and purple cape of Williams College with a
floppy purple hat. He spoke of beginnings: for the graduating
Class of 1956 in their future college careers and for the school
itself as a new Senior Class, my class, with new ideas, talents
and leaders, took its place. He said changes had occurred during the past year, and changes would also occur in the future, as
the boys in the lower classes, each with his own unique talents,
weaknesses and dreams, would interact each day in the future
with the life and traditions of an institution that needed them to
prod it, to make it change and accommodate itself to differences,
and to grow and thrive.

It was as though he was speaking to me. Mr. Stevens was a
conjurer transforming this poorly-endowed school with his
words into the most exciting and important place in the world;
he even managed to divert me for a while from daydreaming
about Joann Sutherland's sly smile. Mr. Stevens' booming voice
kept my attention. He was like a Baptist preacher, with his blazing eyes hugely magnified by those round, steel-rimmed glasses.
He said things like "We will succeed..." and "...our vision of
what our school will be." When he said these things, he wasn't
fooling anybody about what he really meant. He was the school.
Though I liked to think Mr. Stevens was high-minded and sincere, I still had a little residual cynicism in me that made it hard
for me to swallow his sermon. I still could hear Bob Downey's
nasal voice snidely whispering in my ear from the grave—did he

kill himself in that car wreck?—that any adults, and particularly teachers, were incapable of sincerely believing in anything other than the endless exercise of unlimited power over children to feed their illusion of superiority.

As we all left the gym after graduation and were milling around the quadrangle under the trees shaking hands and saying good-bye, have a good summer and things like that, I got a few seniors I liked to write something in my Yearbook. They were writing profound stuff like "look me up next year" at Amherst or Yale or Brown or Stetson or wherever. Mr. Maxwell saw what I was doing and came over to me, took my Yearbook and wrote *Meilleurs souhaits—et voeux —et bonne chance, un peu partout.* I thought it meant "good wishes and good luck in everything" but wasn't sure. Just like him to do it *en francais.* As he would say, *bien sur.*

Chapter Eight

THE SUMMER WENT like blazes. Dad took me to the Ford dealer in Dobbs Ferry and bought me a used 1952 two-door Ford coupe as a delayed sixteenth birthday present. It was black and white, had white leather seats and a chrome band that went from side to side over the roof. It was wonderful and it didn't matter that I wasn't supposed to drive at night or in New York City on my junior license. In fact, it wasn't long before Dad was letting me drive it at night, if not into the City, where I didn't want to go anyway. Being able to take Joann Sutherland to the movies, usually the drive-in in Elmsford, was all I wanted to do, and I did it as often as Joann would go out with me, which was a lot that summer. I thought about Joann often and got all excited whenever I thought about how I'd kissed her and cuddled with her in my sporty Ford. We made plans for her to come to Williston—she went to Pine Manor, a girls' school near Boston—for the Senior

Dance just before graduation next spring. She had a ponytail and deep dimples in her cheeks when she gave me sly smiles. She had a teasing way of kind of half-smiling and looking at me from the corner of her eyes, never straight at me, that made every look seem like an invitation to wild, raw, uninhibited sex. Whatever she was actually thinking when she looked at me like that, I don't think it was wild sex. She wasn't like that. In fact, she liked to kiss a lot, but she wouldn't let me anywhere near her wonderful boobs, swelling up under her blouse or Shetland sweater. The closest I'd ever come to them wasn't when we were kissing in the car, but when we were horsing around in the pool at the Ardsley Country Club and I'd try to accidentally bump into her chest. That hadn't worked either. I guess I wanted to feel Joann's breasts about as much as anything I'd ever wanted to do in this world, at least to that point in my life.

I tried a couple of jobs that summer. The first was selling a local newspaper door-to-door, which turned me off selling anything because I was so bad at it. One of the kids who was very good at it wore his arm in a sling as if it were broken. Whoever answered the door would notice the arm and hesitate from packing him off just long enough to allow him to begin his persuasive spiel about working for his education. Sometimes, if he picked up on his radar that the person was a sports fan, he'd say he broke his arm playing baseball, sliding for home with the winning run. That worked well on men. On women, he'd use another approach —he'd say that things weren't going too well at home. He'd look at the ground and mumble that his father was out of work and sometimes drank too much. He doesn't mean to hurt me, he'd say. That kid was a supersalesman and was supposed to impart his tricks for success to me, but I was a hopeless cause. So, I looked for other work, mindful that the fathers of some of the other kids in Ardsley got them summer jobs in brokerage houses and law firms or their companies. Dad never offered to do that for me, but I wasn't sure I wanted him to. I think he wondered what I could come up with on my own, and what I usually came up with was short.

My next job that summer was at Rosedale Nurseries, a tree nursery in Hawthorne, New York. The first few days, I liked that job. I could drive to work in my excellent black and white Ford with the snazzy chrome band across the top. Mom would pack a brown bag with a sandwich and a banana or an apple and send me off to hoe row after everlasting row of little baby yew trees. That was the bad part. The hoe the nursery gave me was very sharp and the little yew trees very tender. I killed a lot of them —cut them off in their infancy. After two weeks of carnage, I got fired. They didn't pay me and, instead, sent Dad a bill for the difference between my peon wages and the cost of the yew trees I'd killed. It cost dad over $100 to have me work in the blazing sun for two weeks.

He suggested I look for a volunteer job of some kind which might not cost him too much, and so I retired from trying to work for money for the summer. Instead, I became an unpaid volunteer for the American Field Service, meeting groups of teenagers from France, Holland, Italy and Scandinavia at Idlewild Airport and taking them on sightseeing tours around New York City on Circle Line boats. To tell the truth, most of the time I spent ogling a robust girl from Dobbs Ferry who turned out to be the girl named Jewelle that Dr. Kertess talked to. She was also working as a volunteer but I never got to speak to her because she kept taking her groups one way when I had to go another.

MOM DROVE ME up to Williston in early September to begin my senior year. As she drove putting her foot down on the pedal and taking it off, white knuckles and all, I was trying to think only a little about how important this year was for me; it was simply too heavy a subject. It was better, even a little exciting, to think about how great being a senior, and a big wheel senior—Vice President of the Student Council, News Editor of *The Willistonian* and one of Mac's Favored Few—was going to be. And the Dodgers were the World Champs on their way to another National League pennant even though Gil Hodges wasn't doing so great. Maybe Dad was watching him too much. He told me he didn't watch the Dodgers' games on television because he was a jinx.

I thought about all the teachers I'd really gotten to know pretty well last year and pictured them in my mind as if they were all standing together for a photograph. There was Headmaster Stevens in the center, much taller than the others, clearly the leader of the pack, standing in a brown herringbone tweed jacket, medium gray flannels, smiling but with his prophet's eyes blazing through his round, steel-rimmed glasses. At his right hand, appropriately, stood Mac in his blue blazer and a button-down, striped Brooks Brothers shirt. He'd drawn himself up to look as big as possible next to Mr. Stevens, but couldn't pull it off. Mac's blue blazer with the Yale patch and brass buttons was a little too big for his slight build and his smile was a little too tight, a little phony, as though he really didn't want to say

cheese. Mr. Rouse, bald, his gray-white brush mustache matching his gray suit, wearing a big bow tie and his chipmunk grin,
was next to Mac on the far right. On Mr. Stevens' left stood Mr.
Hepworth, tank-like, erect, radiating energy, holding his ever-
present pipe, his fierce eyes burning like hot coals. He wasn't
smiling. In fact, he looked like J.P. Morgan Jr. in a photograph
Mr. Hepworth had shown us the previous year. The picture was
taken during a Congressional hearing in 1933 when a midget sat
on Morgan's lap at the behest of a circus publicist. Morgan's eyes
were blazing.

There were others, of course, in the background of my mental
photograph: teachers, coaches, the school nurse, the town librarian, Helen and Boris at DeBarbieri's, classmates, especially Bruce
Eldridge and Steve David. Among all those images, mostly I fo-
cused on Mr. Maxwell and me and wondered what adventures in
New York or Northampton were in store for me with him. Also
beginning this fall, I would be given the grand privilege of being
allowed to hang out in the living room of Mac's suite on the top
floor of Ford Hall, the senior dormitory, aware of the envy of all
those who were not welcome there, which was almost everybody
except a few of us—Tom Mickle, who had been at the concert
in Northampton last year, and Preston Peters, "Joe" Hine, John
Hutchinson and "Tiger" Revson from Greenwich—preppies all.
While none of them were my best friends, we liked each other
and understood that we shared a common bond—we now were
the Favored Few.

I spent more time in Mac's room than at DeBarbieri's in town
with Bruce and Steve and my other pals that fall, because something good was always going on there. There was a pot of coffee

on a hotplate, sometimes doughnuts filched from the kitchen, and always *The New Yorker* and other new magazines, and *The New York Times* every day, so I read about Gil Hodges and the Dodgers in the fall as they lost the World Series to the damn Yankees again in seven games. Mac's door was always open and the Favored Few were free to come and go whether or not he was there. It was usually pretty quiet if he wasn't around, and, Mr. Maxwell's room being the only place on campus we were allowed to watch television, someone might turn on the set. If he was there, we'd talk about things he liked—new plays on Broadway, his plans for going to France the next summer and the friends he was going to stay with—a writer in Provençe and a painter with a villa near St. Tropez.

Mac liked art and knew a lot about it. He was excited by all the noise about artists named Pollock, de Kooning and Rothko— some of his favorites, he said—which were being shown at the Tate in London that fall. He loved laughing about people, such as the veteran teacher with a permanently crossed eye and the scrawny young teacher with ears that stuck out so far we thought he should stay indoors on windy days. He invented an elaborate, imaginary affair for the sexy young wife of a new, young teacher, who couldn't hide her despair at being stuck in Easthampton, with "Pepe," a mythical, handsome and horny Spanish grounds keeper from Honduras, who no one ever saw because he was always too exhausted to show up for work.

Maxwell's room was the place where jokes were told and where we got all the news of the school. "The $64,000 Question" was an intense weekly event that fall on television. We had groaned and screamed the previous year as Dr. Joyce Brothers, the love-object of most normal types, displayed her incredible range of knowledge in the sweaty isolation booth and won the jackpot. This year's contestants weren't as interesting, although a seventy-five-year-old woman on public assistance won on her amazing knowledge of Dickens. But, blonde and brainy Joyce Brothers, she wasn't.

Bruce Eldridge was my roommate. We flipped a dime to see who'd get the favored bottom bunk and I lost. He wasn't happy about how much time I spent in Mr. Maxwell's room and the fact that he wasn't welcome there, but he built a radio from scratch from old parts and that kept him busy. All in all, life was terrific for me. After the first marking period ended at the Thanksgiving break, I was number two in my class, only a whisker from number one, David Montague, and only a whisker ahead of Steve David. Although Montague was a total and obnoxious grind, I liked him, but, of course, I wanted to kill him, too.

I was Vice President of the Student Council through the intervention of a benevolent Providence since the Vice President didn't have to speak publicly unless the President, Forbes Warren, got sick, which he didn't, thanks, no doubt, to my constant prayers for his good health. My job as News Editor of *The Willistonian* took a lot of time every week, much of which was spent in Mac's room since he read all the copy that went in the newspaper and changed a lot because he had definite opinions about everything, even the layout.

I sang in the Glee Club and kept my grades up enough to be inducted into the Cum Laude Society later in the year. I was on a roll. By Christmas, Steve David, Dave Montague and I were at the top of our class, sending Montague into spasms of all-night, flashlight-under-the-blanket cram sessions, sure to ruin his weak, beady little eyes.

"Don't you ever do anything else?" I asked him. "Don't you ever think of something other than studying, like raw naked sex with Marilyn Monroe or something healthy and normal like that?"

"Sure I do," he replied resentfully. "Just like the rest of you assholes, only I do it better."

"How so, greasy Grind? Your roomie there says he never once has heard your sheets go kerthunk-kerthunk." His roommate nodded agreement.

"True, you poor, limited, disgusting cretin; I think off!" he sneered, sure that he'd trumped me with this incredible feat of pure intellect. And, godammit, he had. It was fun to try, but I wondered if he really could do it because I couldn't; neither could Bruce who thought it might not be scientifically possible. Failure at anything made me feel mediocre, but I knew that's what Montague wanted me to feel, so I didn't tell him. I must admit that I treated him with a little more respect after that, a worthy opponent in our unfinished match for the title, but he was still a Grind.

During the Christmas vacation, I joined Maxwell twice for theater outings in the City. By then Marian McPartland recognized me and smiled and seemed real happy to see us when we showed up for drinks at the Mayan Room in Rockefeller Center where she was playing. It felt good when she recognized me, as if I was a regular friend of hers.

Mac was trying to get me to read some novels by a woman, Mary Renault, he said he'd discovered. There were three of them, all about life in ancient Greece, and all of them looked like they had a couple of thousand pages and weighed about five pounds. I really wasn't all that interested in life in ancient Greece that Christmas—Joann's boobs, definitely, but not Greeks who liked boys a lot, according to Mr. Maxwell. Anyway, I didn't read the books, but didn't want to tell Mr. Maxwell I hadn't read any of them because I knew he'd be disappointed in me. So, while it was a little hard to bluff my way through conversations with him about them, he didn't ask too many questions and told me a lot about them, so I was able to muddle through okay. He was always trying to get me to read something, but I usually had enough to read on my own.

Mom and Dad were pretty happy that Christmas about the way things were going for me, but didn't know what to make of my theater outings in the City with Mr. Maxwell. I guess they found it a little hard to believe that a teacher could really like doing things like that with a kid, but they didn't know Mac, or any other teacher, for that matter. They'd always wondered about why Dr. Kertess was interested in me, so now they had two things to wonder about. Anyway, they seemed happy that I was going to the theater and were really happy about my grades. They could hardly believe I was doing so well—maybe, I'd get into Keokuk A&M yet. I even earned a pat on the head from Dad. "Seems you're doing okay up there now. Maybe, you're just a late bloomer," he'd said, at least noticing that, maybe, I was blooming. Maybe there was hope for me yet. Maybe.

Shortly after the Christmas vacation, Fred L. Glimp came to Williston. Fred L. Glimp was a roving admissions officer who had the power, which he could exercise right on the spot, if he so chose, to grant admission to Harvard College. He must have ridden into town on his palomino stallion wearing a big, white ten-gallon Stetson—a one-man cavalry able to render quick justice from the point of his pencil. He was, of course, one of the Most Important People on Earth and I penciled in my name on the sign-up sheet to see him.

Now, the thought of going to Harvard, which had been pretty well squashed under Chilson Leonard's foot, seemed completely unreal to me. I was headed for someplace else, maybe a college in Florida or Southern California where I could bask in the sun and not be bothered too much that I didn't have a future. However, there was that fragile little bud of residual life that had survived and had been unfolding more and more from the nutrients of the intervening year and a third at Williston, or I wouldn't have even bothered to sign up. I wrote my name on the list under Steve David's, but, as soon as I'd done it, I knew that the little bud was not yet ready to be seen by the august personage of Fred L. Glimp. So, I tried to erase my name, which didn't work very well and I wound up crossing it out with a pencil.

I'd noticed on the sign-up sheet that there were only two other seniors who had the nerve to think they might be candidates for Harvard: Montague, the Grind, who would undoubtedly be accepted on the spot, and my pal Steve David—lustful, obscene, salivating dreamer of mammoth, pendulous breasts and hairy, sweaty, straining loins whose brain was in an around-the-clock war with his penis for possession of his soul. He'd told me about his spending every summer, every vacation during the school year and even long weekends, in Washington, D.C., where he lived, selling Muntz TVs door-to-door. He did this not only to make money, at which he truly excelled, but also to get into the boudoirs of lonely housewives and horny Government secretaries and the chance to score, at which he said he also succeeded brilliantly. I wondered about that because I didn't know anybody who scored much, if at all.

I thought that Steve's chances of getting into Harvard were pretty good, assuming there were no females anywhere near during his interview with Fred L. Glimp. On the other hand, if there was anything remotely feminine—of any kind, height, girth or age—nearby, I could honestly see Steve interrupting the Exalted Glimp in mid-sentence, learning toward him conspiratorially and blurting out, with a salacious leer, as he had with me a thousand times, "Hey, Fred, tell me, ain't that some *pussy?*"

The actual day that the Excellent Glimp arrived went very slowly for me. I knew that Steve had a morning appointment with him, but I didn't know the rest of his schedule. I desperately wanted that day over so that I could stop lashing myself for not having the courage to see him.

As I was on the way into the dining hall for lunch, Mr. Stevens caught my arm from behind and guided me to his own table, the Head Table, of course. I saw a stranger standing there in a tweed sport jacket and I knew this could be none other than Fred L. Glimp. As Stevens recited the blessing on our food and dedicated us to the Will and Service of God on the loudspeaker system, as he did three times a day, I noted that there were only two other students at the table, Montague and Steve David. Maxwell was there and so were Mr. Hepworth and my doting English teacher, Mr. Rouse. Mrs. Stevens, with her enormous matronly bosom and her graying hair in a severe bun, looking grandmotherly before her time in a frumpy cotton dress, was also bowing her head in prayer over the reconstituted gray mashed potatoes and the slightly grayer mystery meat. Her presence virtually ensured that Steve would spend the entire meal in misery, trying to conceal his hard-on. Before Mr. Stevens had even finished saying grace, Steve had whispered to me out of the corner of his mouth: "Sweet Jesus, Bumppo," he slathered, "can you believe those tits?"

After the Amen, and I had actually shaken the hand of Fred L. Glimp, Mr. Stevens started talking about what a great place Harvard was, almost as good as Williams (Stevens' college— ho ho). Mr. Glimp seemed relaxed and friendly and Stevens, Hepworth, Maxwell and Rouse said they were really proud of the three of us.

I squirmed when Mr. Rouse gushed to Mr. Glimp that I was one of the finest students he'd ever taught. Good grief! Mr. Stevens said how pleased he was that the three top students in the senior class all were thinking of going to Harvard. Good grief again! He obviously didn't know that I'd crossed out my name. I was sure that I needed to say something to correct the mistake, still, I was too lily-livered to force an opening, and none just happened. I looked at the Magnificent Glimp, who must have known that my name was crossed off the list, for some sign that he knew my being there was a mistake. There was no sign. What would happen when he found out? Should I go through with it, and pretend that someone else had crossed out my name as a sick joke?

I pictured Glimp, not as Roy Rogers on his trusty palomino

saving the good guys, but as Genghis Glimp sitting cross-legged, wrapped in an enormous black kimono embellished with crimson dragons, each hand thrust into the opposite flowing sleeve, slits for eyes, a drooping Fu Manchu moustache and a wispy beard, silent, still, unmoving, all-knowing. Then, in a split-second flash the human eye could not follow, Genghis Glimp sprang up from the table, screamed "Eiii…" and decapitated me with one lightning stroke of his ancient, blood-soaked scimitar. He hacked at my headless body a few times hissing "Presumptuous Pig!" and then sat down again to eat.

Despite my mental diversions, I couldn't help getting involved in the discussion at the table. Didn't I know something about Harvard from my older brother—hadn't he just graduated last year?—and from my father, Mr. Stevens asked? Sure I did, but I really didn't want to get into talking about Harvard a whole lot since I knew I wasn't going there, but I simply couldn't not say anything. So, I told them that Bob had liked it a lot at Harvard and so had my father, who still did a lot of alumni things for his class and wouldn't miss a reunion. But, I didn't say much and let the others do most of the talking.

After lunch, the Omnipotent Glimp came around the table to me. He said that he had some time available since his next appointment was not until three thirty; if I wanted, we could have more than an hour to chat. Like a wimp, I said, hardly able to breathe, sure, why not? I could do that. So we walked into the cozy, pine-paneled lounge next to the dining room that was usually full of faculty members but had been given over for this day exclusively to Fred L. Glimp.

We sat facing each other on two green Naugahyde sofas before a small fire and talked until after three o'clock. He had a white manila folder with my name on it, but seemed to know a lot about me without looking at the folder. He knew that my cousin Tim had gone to Harvard, that Bob had majored in Government there and had been in the Glee Club, and that Dad was in the Class of 1924. He said that when my name had been given to him several weeks before by Phil Stevens as having signed up for an interview, he'd been given my transcripts from Exeter as well as my grades at Williston. He said Mr. Stevens had written him a note asking him to compare the huge difference between my records at the two schools. Was there a way for Glimp to look into the Exeter problem, Stevens had asked—not because Williston was worried about it, that wasn't the case—but to prevent Harvard from being misled by what appeared to be a strange mistake at Exeter?

Mr. Glimp told me that he'd gotten to know Bill Saltonstall, the Principal of Exeter, quite well from his rounds of the New England prep schools and that he'd visited Exeter two weeks before. "So Chilson Leonard was your English II teacher?" he asked, although he knew that from my transcripts.

"Yes, sir, he was," I said.

"Do you remember your grade for the first half year?"

"Not exactly, but it was in the high 80's."

"87," he said looking at a manila folder. "Do you remember your grade for the whole year?"

"Yes, sir. I sure do. I'll never forget it. It was 59."

"So your average for the second half of the year had to have been, what...32? How did you manage to get a 32 on even one English paper? What happened?"

"Oh, I got some much lower than that," I answered. "I got a 27 on one long paper I worked on pretty hard. I never did figure out how he graded."

Glimp had a serious expression on his round face as I gave a short version of what happened to me at Exeter. He asked me a lot of questions like what did my parents say about the whole thing? What did I feel about it then? What do I feel about it now? I told him I thought I was getting over it here at Williston and that I would surely survive, even if Dad had doubts, trying to make it sound funny. At the end, Mr. Glimp leaned back into the Naugahyde sofa, stretched out his legs and stared up at the ceiling.

"I know Chilson Leonard, not well, but I've spoken to him several times on my various trips to Exeter," he said. "He's something of an odd duck: half woodsman, half poet. He's obviously a man who's used to being alone with an axe or a gun or a book. He seems to scowl all the time—pretty hard to warm up to or even talk to. 'Glum' is a good word for him."

Glimp, indeed, knew the man. "Yes, sir, that's Leonard alright," I agreed.

"But what he did to you is one of the most vicious things I've ever heard of. It makes me shudder," said the Truly Excellent Glimp with feeling. He sat up abruptly, as if he'd just decided something.

"I want you to know that I think you should apply to Harvard and that if you keep up your record here through the next term, I can promise you that you will be accepted. I will see to it."

The All-Powerful Glimp had spoken! Such beautiful words! Words I truly thought I'd never hear! I wanted to say something, but my throat was so tight and my mind so stupidly empty that I couldn't say a single word, not even "thanks." I sat there, dumb and staring at Glimp. Glimp could see that I was all choked up, so he decided to end the embarrassing silence.

"You'll want to think about it, I'm sure. Maybe you've made some other plans. Just let me know if you decide to go ahead so I can track your application."

"I will. And, Mr. Glimp, thanks," I finally managed. "You know I'd decided not to try—"

"I know. The sign-up sheet," he interrupted.

" —because I didn't think I had a chance."

"You do have a chance, actually more than just a chance. I'm telling you now that you will be accepted unless you foul up in the next few months and I'm willing to bet that you won't. Your record here under the circumstances is almost miraculous. The way I've been lobbied by Stevens, Maxwell, Rouse and Arch Hepworth—he got his MA at Harvard, you know—is most unusual. I shouldn't even count Chuck Rouse who must either be a close relative or on your payroll. Seriously, what I'm constantly looking for is the boy who's growing. There always will be places at Harvard for boys who are so brilliant that they have always gotten straight A's in everything. However, the ones who are exciting to me, and who make Harvard exciting, are the ones who started somewhere else and brought themselves up, the ones who faced a challenge and succeeded. While I can't remember another case just like yours, thank God, I do know that you faced a serious challenge, a fundamental challenge, and you are much stronger for it, believe me. Yes, we want you at Harvard."

I left The Incomparable Glimp giddy with uncontrollable

energy. Maybe, I'll run over to the Chapel, I thought. I'd never prayed to get into Harvard, because it just seemed that I'd be asking too much, and I was leery of asking God for things for myself anyway, but I sure felt like going to the Chapel and praying now. Mr. Glimp's words were like the answer to a prayer I'd wanted to make, but even though I hadn't, maybe God knew about it anyway. I wanted to thank Him, but was really just too agitated to sit still in the empty Chapel all by myself. No, I needed to talk to someone. Call Mom and Dad? No, what if I screw up and don't get in after all—better not to tell them anything. I wondered if Dad would have a clue about how I was feeling. Probably not. I remembered the silent trip home from Exeter after Mr. Leonard's last English class. Dad didn't seem really mad at anyone but me—not furious at Mr. Leonard, like Glimp was. Call Bob? I thought he might take the edge off it, somehow—like saying "big deal" or that Harvard wasn't really so great after all. I didn't want him to spoil it. No, I needed to jump around a little bit and make some noise and give the big old finger to Chilson Leonard, wherever he was. So, I soared back to Mr. Maxwell's room to tell him and whoever of the Favored Few was there all about Fred L. Glimp and these extraordinary happenings. Mr. Maxwell would understand.

By the time I got there, imagining all the way how Chilson Leonard might look choking to death when he heard the news, the spots that always came before a bad migraine headache had begun to blind me. That had happened before when I was really happy about something. It was as if I just couldn't let myself be really, really happy about myself. For me, those migraine episodes became God's way of keeping my feet on the ground or cutting me down to size when my head was getting too swelled up, or something like that. It sure worked that way, whether God was involved or not. So, I didn't stop in at Mr. Maxwell's and went straight to my room and collapsed on my bed, waiting for the spots to blind me completely before they would begin to dissipate and the pounding, throbbing, stabbing pain would come. As the winter grew colder and bleaker and the days darker, my life became brighter and happier. I was doing what I wanted to do most of the time and was doing pretty well at most of those things. I felt privileged to have the obvious goodwill of Mr. Maxwell—he'd really become my best friend—and now my future had been restored by Fred L. Glimp, although I hadn't told anyone about that, not even Mr. Maxwell, not yet. I had a secret; if I told anybody, it might vanish. All I had to do was keep out of trouble. Keeping my nose clean wasn't hard anymore since I almost never even wanted to do anything that was particularly risky. Even the bells stopped jangling my nerves. I wasn't going to let anything stop that letter from Harvard being sent in April. I thought of Mr. Stevens' speech at graduation the previous June about commencements being beginnings. Horseshit! That letter was IT, the end of everything, the beginning of nothing. Clearly my life would stop and my soul would rise to Heaven at the very instant I held it in my hand because there would be nothing better, brighter or more beautiful left for me to achieve on Earth.

PAUL ELKINS, A BOY I'd known only for a few months since he'd come to Williston only for his senior year, got sick toward the end of January. He went into the Infirmary sneezing and coughing and on Sunday, January 27, he died. We were told at the assembly of the whole school on Monday morning. It was a real shock. How could that happen so quickly? Or at all? We were left wondering about it, even after we'd been told that he'd had a form of pneumonia they couldn't stop. Phil Stevens said that he'd decided to suspend classes for the rest of the week and resume the normal schedule the following week.

Most of the students lived fairly nearby and went home. Many of the rest went skiing at Stowe, Killington or Mad River Glen or visited relatives or friends. I didn't want to go home and sit around with Mom and Dad, and decided instead to stay at school for that week, even though the dormitory halls were left eerily quiet, the dining room ghostly, the gymnasium and classroom buildings dark and locked. I needed to finish off all the essays required by the colleges I wanted to apply to—Harvard, of course, but also Brown and maybe some others, in case Fred L. Glimp was not as all-powerful as I'd thought. Those applications required serious and time-consuming effort which I'd neglected until it was almost too late.

However pressed I felt about the applications and mystified by the death of a classmate, I also felt that staying at school and applying myself with such dedication to duty deserved a small reward, especially a reward that would take me away from the dismal, funereal atmosphere of the deserted campus.

I'd seen Sandy Durkee, a Smith freshman I knew from home, on the street in Northampton. Despite the chasm that separates high school seniors from college freshmen, especially girl freshmen, she'd promised to take me on a visit to the forbidden and notorious Rahar's, a phony German beer hall whose prosperity derived from its policy that anyone tall and strong enough to open its door must be at least twenty-one years old, the legal drinking age in Massachusetts. However, since absolutely no one there—and it was jammed every night—was in fact of legal age, and its atmosphere was dense with stale beer, staler smoke and loud music, professors and teachers from all of the surrounding schools and colleges in the area never went there, observing the unwritten protocol that such places should be allowed to flourish in college towns. For me even to cross its threshold was a capital offense, a risk I'd carefully avoided taking, at least until then. With the campus so deserted, the omens seemed propitious. Mr. Maxwell said he was going to Chicago, where his mother lived, so I didn't have to worry about bumping into him that Saturday night with beer on my breath. I called Sandy and she said it would be fun and we made a date for Wednesday night.

Still, I was scared. Part of me recognized that I was so close to the end that taking a big risk now was just plain stupid. But, another other part of me was determined to go to Rahar's, a potentially self-destructive impulse that had me increasingly nervous and perplexed. What was this strange compulsion to do something risky? What about my vow to do nothing that could stop that letter from Harvard? Was some self-created demon trying to derail me again so close to the goal line, maybe, to prove to Dad that I was a failure with no future after all? Whatever its source, that impulse overcame my good judgment. Although I knew that taking this chance was incredibly stupid, I was going to do it.

I played with the idea of using a disguise, like a wig or a false mustache, but I couldn't figure out how to come up with something that wouldn't attract attention and make me look ludicrous, not to mention the problem of explaining it to Sandy, my Smithie date. So, in the end, I decided to take my chances and plunge ahead, facially naked.

I spent all day Tuesday and Wednesday morning grinding away on my college applications trying to find interesting ways to answer questions like: "What books, other than any book assigned for reading in any of your courses this year, have you: (a) read, (b) enjoyed, and (c) why?" Another beaut was: "What is the most important thing that ever happened to you?"

My first efforts to write brilliant and insightful answers left me in panic. I just couldn't produce anything but silly drivel. I spent a lot of time with my feet up staring out my top floor window in Ford Hall at the deserted quadrangle below in the cold, thin winter sun. Since my mind was about as empty as the campus, I decided to go "downtown" to DeBarbieri's where I was sure to find Helen. She'd take my mind off my problems by telling me all about her latest crisis—and there was always a crisis. Perhaps Helen's latest crisis, or listening to Dean Martin sing "Memories Are Made of This" for the zillionth time, would dredge up some event—anything other than Exeter and Chilson Leonard—to write about as my Most Important Thing, although Mr. Leonard definitely topped the list.

Unfortunately, all of the episodes that came to mind as I walked through the cold, deserted campus toward DeBarbieri's were not of the sort that I wanted any college admissions person to know, such as killing Mom's Rambler or the Battle of the Rough Rider Room. Those would hardly inspire confidence in my character. Neither would my own Most Important Thing at the moment, which was Getting Laid, but as that had not happened yet, all

I could do—and did a lot—was dream about it. There wasn't even an outside chance of getting lucky with Sandy, the Smithie, was there? My hands became sweaty in my fur-lined gloves as I wondered what Sandy was doing right then. What was she thinking? Probably she was sorry that she'd got herself into a date with a prep school kid. What was Joann Sutherland doing right then? My hands got sweatier when I thought of Joann's silky brown ponytail and dimples and her sly, hot looks and wonderful boobs. She said she would go to the big Spring Dance at Williston with me in May, which seemed so far away it would never come. Would Joann think my date with Sandy was treason? After all, Joann had given me her Dana Hall ring and I'd given her my blue and gold Williston senior ring and all that was supposed to mean something. Anyhow, Sandy was just a pal and how would Joann ever find out? Does she even know Sandy? Maybe. The more I thought about it, the more I knew that, for sure, nothing was going to happen with Sandy.

I did try to keep my mind on coming up with something I could write about as my Most Important Thing, like showing New York City to kids from all over Europe for the American Field Service. Maybe I could make enough of one of the experiences I had doing that to show that I was really a Good Citizen, omitting the information that by far the most interesting sights to the European kids, particularly the girls, was not the Empire State Building or the Statue of Liberty, but all the funny, long, white eely things (*poissons blanc* I bet Mr. Maxwell would call them) floating in great numbers in the East River.

As my luck would have it, Helen was out sick or bruised or something and the place was empty, except for Boris, who had unplugged the juke box and whose eyes made it clear that it could be dangerous to plug it back in or even to stay there. My problem unsolved, I ambled back in the cold gloom towards the campus.

As I passed Mr. Maxwell's door and the head of the stairs in the middle of the top floor of Ford Hall, I saw the door open, the living room empty. Strange. I thought he'd gone to see his mother in Chicago. I stuck my head in and called "Mac" and "Anyone home?" Silence. I called again, and was about to leave when I heard Mr. Maxwell's voice coming from the bedroom at the end of a narrow corridor off the living room. He moaned my name twice, "Bumppo…Bumppo…" and sounded like he was in great pain. Although I'd never been down that corridor to his bedroom before, I didn't hesitate because it seemed clear that something was wrong. Maybe he'd had a heart attack or a stroke.

I charged down the dark passageway and, just as I emerged into the dimly lit bedroom not knowing what to expect, Mr. Maxwell grabbed me in an embrace, pinning my arms to my sides, and kissed me on the mouth. I felt his hands grope down to my balls and he began to moan, "Bumppo, I love you…I love you…" I stared wide-eyed into his face an inch from mine. His skin was glistening with sweat and he hadn't shaved. He smelled terrible and his eyes were wild. He looked as if he'd gone completely insane.

How I got out of there, and whether I said anything to him, I don't remember. Somehow I got back to my own room at the corner of that floor of Ford Hall. I climbed onto my upper bunk and shut my eyes, hoping that the memory would be totally obliterated. What just happened hadn't happened at all. I was seeing things again or dreaming or someone would tell me it was just a terrible joke—anything, anything at all, to explain away what had happened.

I could feel the brittle little cocoon of hope and confidence I'd built around me at Williston break and crumble in seconds. It was all a delusion! Just like the spots I saw before a migraine started, or the colors I "saw" at the concert, I had been seeing things that really weren't there. And, worse, the truth was right in front of my face. The theater outings in New York became obscene. What a gullible idiot I was! He never liked me. Those books—about the Greeks and their boys! Idiot! Idiot! I just didn't get it. Of course he wasn't interested in Maggie the "Cat." Imbecile!

My future—not only the dim, misty far-away fantasy of Harvard but also the future of that very evening's meal and that night and the next morning and the next—seemed unimaginable. I simply couldn't imagine myself going through the routine of another day there, but had no idea of what else I could do. Do I tell anyone about it? How can I? How can't I? I've got to talk to someone, but who? Who can I possibly trust? Who will believe me? What about Harvard? What will happen? To me? To him? Will they believe me? Will I have to leave Williston? Yes, Yes. No, I can't. Not now. Not so close to the end!

I tossed on my bunk, got up, sat down, got up on the bed again, and began hearing Maxwell's voice, clear and distinct, moaning inside my ear, coming from inside my brain, "Bumppo, I love you... I love you..." The voice followed me and rose and fell, sometimes whispering, sometimes screaming in my ear, drowning out everything else, sometimes eerie and distorted like a 78 record on 33 1/3 RPM, always moaning the same thing, "I love you… I love you…" A paralysis came over me slowing my spastic movements and eventually making any movement at all extraordinarily difficult without intense concentration. I looked at my hands but couldn't move them.

Convinced that maybe I was actually losing my mind, my grip on life itself uncertain—as I considered the four-story drop below my windows and tried to imagine what I'd look like if I dove out headfirst onto the concrete pavement—the risks and dangers of finding someone to talk to faded away. I had to talk to someone. Hepworth. Robust Hepworth. Masculine Hepworth. Happily married Hepworth. I would go to see him, now, at his house. Hope to God he is there. Mr. Hepworth will know what to do.

Putting on my boots and loden coat with its wooden pegs and leather thongs was an agony of frustration and effort since my fingers didn't work, but not as hard as simply turning the doorknob on the door to the corridor to the stairs through which I must go, passing by the door to Mr. Maxwell's room, open and yawning in my mind's eye, waiting to swallow me up. My fingers were numb and useless, hanging on my deadweight hands, but I managed to turn the knob, open the door a crack and peer down the corridor. Although I couldn't be sure, it seemed as if Mr. Maxwell's door was shut. I ran down the corridor, past his door—it was shut—and hurled myself down the three flights of stairs, out of Ford Hall and into the cold shock of the bleak afternoon, amazed that so much time had gone by then that the sun had almost disappeared. I ran hunched against the cold through the campus, heart thumping, down the street leading to Mr.

Hepworth's small white frame house where he lived alone with his wife, a thin and remote gray-haired woman I knew nothing about. I did know that the Hepworths had a son who had been killed in the Korean War and that there was a sadness, a profound loneliness, about her and that house. She answered the door.

I was shown into the parlor, as she called it, and invited to sit in a blue overstuffed armchair with a neat white antimacassar. Mr. Hepworth, in a brown cardigan sweater with leather buttons and his usual bow tie, sat at one end of a matching blue sofa, with an antimacassar behind each of the three seats. Between the couch and my chair was a glass coffee table piled high with magazines, books, letters, a pipe stand with six different pipes, a can of tobacco, and lots of other things. A glass martini shaker, half full, was sitting on top of a stack of books; Mr. Hepworth's half empty cone-shaped glass was next to it.

I told him as quickly as I could what had happened. Mr. Hepworth had a deep crease in the middle of his forehead that I'd seen appear many times before, usually when someone's stupidity or ineptitude exceeded his comprehension. The crease appeared now and I was sure its cause was utter disgust for me. He'd probably either call me a fairy or a liar and, in either case, throw me out. I wiped my mouth for the hundredth time.

"Have you told your parents about this?" he asked.

"No, sir."

"I think you should do that. Call them from here," he said pointing to a telephone on a side table next to my chair. "Tell them that you spoke to me and that I think you should go home, now, tonight, and stay home as long as you want to. I'll explain your absence to the Headmaster. As for Maxwell, I really don't know…" He stroked his chin, deep in thought.

Okay, I said, still not knowing if he thought I was lying. I called home, forgetting to reverse the charges, and reached Mom. I told her I wanted to come home right away, that it was hard to explain why on the phone. Fine, she said, a little surprised, but not asking me for an explanation. While I was speaking, Mrs. Hepworth handed me a schedule of the trains to New York from Springfield. We went over the schedule and Mom suggested, a little tipsy already, that I take the train to Stamford, Connecticut, that arrived there at nine thirty that night and take a taxi home from there. She would pay for the taxi. Did I have enough money for the train? Yes, I said, wishing with all my might that she would suddenly, magically, appear right then in the Hepworths' living room and hug me and say everything would be alright, wishing she would at least offer to pick me up at the train station, wishing that I could replay the film of my life during the entire past four years in fast reverse. I knew that by nine thirty that night Mom couldn't pick me up at the train station because she would be too drunk to drive anywhere, maybe even to talk, and she knew it, too. The train left for New York in less than an hour and it would take most of that time to get to the Springfield station since the roads were icy and dangerous.

"Do you have to go back to your room for anything?" Mr. Hepworth asked. No, I didn't, not wanting to go back there for anything in the world.

The crease deepened. "I can't drive you to the train. I'd like to, but I can't." he said. "Too many of these." He picked up his glass, drained it and filled it up again from the shaker. "Her, too," he said, filling up the glass Mrs. Hepworth had held out to him without a word.

"That's fine...I don't want to bother you...I'm really sorry I've bothered you...I'm sorry. I'm really sorry," I stammered, not having any idea of how I could get to the train station and staggered by the news that this strong man into whose hands I had virtually placed my life was too soused to drive his car. He didn't look drunk and he certainly didn't sound drunk, not like my Night Mother anyway. Then I noticed that Mr. Hepworth hadn't moved from his seat on the couch and I guessed that, maybe, he couldn't stand up.

"You aren't bothering us. I am very, very sorry for what's happened to you," Mr. Hepworth said solemnly. He clearly didn't think I was lying, and why would I have come to him if I was a fairy? Mrs. Hepworth suddenly returned from nowhere. "I called a man in town who sometimes drives us places," she announced too precisely. "He'll be here in a few minutes."

"Thank you...thanks so much," I said, getting up too soon. "I really don't want to be so much trouble for you...I'm so sorry for all of this."

Mr. Hepworth told me to sit down. "You aren't any trouble, I told you," he said, but nicely. Now I wanted to talk about it, to understand what happened, but I couldn't start and Mr. Hepworth didn't say anything. An agony of embarrassed silence came over all three of us. Should we chat about the weather? None of us said anything until we heard the car arrive and the horn honk.

I DON'T REMEMBER the trip home—not the man who drove me to the train, not getting on the train, not what I thought about during the trip, not anything about the taxi ride home. I do remember Mom's lurching, worried, groping hug and her gin-breath, an odor that revolted me. I also remember that Dad was in better shape, but still more than normally affected by his usual three Imperial whiskies—had he had more that night? He looked very serious and somber, as though someone died, even before he'd heard anything about what had happened. I guess he was sure that I'd screwed up again. Another problem with Bumppo.

I've always had difficulty telling my parents, particularly Dad, the whole truth about anything. I didn't think he could handle it very well. I couldn't predict what he would do with it and found, through painful experience, that he usually did the wrong thing. Telling Mom anything of importance at this point in her nightly journey into oblivion was pointless. So, hoping to get through it as quickly as possible, I told them that Mr. Maxwell had "made a pass" at me and that I didn't want to stay at school for a while because of it. I felt really tired and hoped that would be enough for them then. "Can we talk about it tomorrow? I'm really bushed."

"No, sir!" Dad said, his eyes red-rimmed and blazing. "What do you mean that he 'made a pass' at you? What in hell does that mean?" he screamed.

"He kissed me," I said, mortified.

"Is that all? Did he do anything else?" Dad's voice was now cold and clinical.

"He said he loved me," I answered, full of shame and embarrassment.

"Now is that it? Was there anything else—anything at all?" I struggled for a long minute. "He felt me. Down there."

My stomach churned and I swallowed metallic—tasting sa-
liva. I ran upstairs to my bathroom and threw up. When I looked
up from kneeling over the toilet bowl, shaking and clammy with
cold sweat, Dad was standing in the open doorway.

"I'm going to drive you back there tomorrow morning, so you
better get some sleep. We'll see about your fairy teacher!" he said
with disgust as he stormed off.

The next day, in the car going back to Williston, I didn't ask
Dad what he was going to do when we got back to school. I
didn't have a clue, but I didn't ask. I was numb, on automatic
pilot, functioning but trying not to think. After an hour or so
of driving in silence, Dad began to question me. He asked me
to tell him about it: What time did it happen? Where? Describe
the passageway. Describe Maxwell's bedroom. Had I been there
before? Surely, I must have been there before. Did I sit on the
bed? Was the bed made? What color was the bedspread? Was
the window shade down? What did Maxwell say? Repeat every
single word he said. What did he look like? What did he smell
like? Had he been drinking? What was he wearing? Did he have
his pants on? Did he have an erection? Was his prick out of his
pants? Did I touch it? Tell the truth! I put it in my mouth, didn't
I? Tell the truth! Where was I standing? What did I do? Tell the
truth! Did I fight him? Hit him? Smash him in the face? Why
not? Insult him? Why not? Come on, what did I do? Just stand
there? I must have done something. Tell me the truth! He'd done
it before, hadn't he? Tell the truth. Hadn't he done it before?
Those plays you said you went to with him in the City—what
was I really doing? Tell the truth! Didn't I know he was a queer?
How couldn't I know? I'd been in his bedroom before, hadn't I?

Others were involved too, weren't they? Who else was involved? Damn it, he screamed, TELL THE TRUTH!

Over and over, he asked, shouted, demanded answers. If I changed a word, he seized on it as if I'd admitted something; if I didn't change anything in the second, third or fourth answer to the same question, he asked me how many times I'd rehearsed the answer. Then, after he was exhausted, his knuckles white on the black steering wheel of our car, he said quietly, sadly even: "Isn't it true that you are this teacher's little fairy?" he almost spit. "Isn't that true?"

The words burned like acid. "No, no, for God sakes, no. Dad, it's not true!" I moaned, knowing that I'd just suffered an injury that would last a lifetime. I couldn't stop the tears in my eyes, and my heart.

"I had to ask," he said quietly, but not saying if he believed me. We spent the next two hours in total silence, staring at the road.

When we arrived at Williston, Dad told me to get out of the car at the Hepworths' house and to wait for him there. I was happy to get out of that car, grateful that I would not be forced to see Mr. Maxwell or to witness whatever was going to happen, a scene I could not really imagine since I didn't know what in the world Dad planned to do. I watched as he drove the car slowly toward Ford Hall. Then I began walking aimlessly toward the campus, kicking leftover leaves in the snow, not wanting to intrude on the Hepworths.

Ford Hall wasn't very far away, so I could see our car stop in front of the dormitory. I watched Dad get out and march angrily through the front door. Would he shout and scream? Punch Mr.

Maxwell out? Dad seemed mad enough. Was he really capable of that? Would Mr. Maxwell defend himself? Lie? Beat Dad up? He'd been a soldier and, maybe, he was tougher than he looked. Would Mr. Maxwell cringe and admit it? Or, worse, would he scoff at the whole thing and accuse me of lying or, worse, being the pervert? What if Mr. Maxwell did do something like that to protect himself? He was powerful. He was the Assistant Headmaster, for heaven's sake, respected, well liked, admired. He was Mr. Stevens' right arm! Against this, I was nothing; of no value compared to that excellent man of genuine, solid accomplishment. Who would believe me? Not even my own father.

Dad bolted out the battered front door of Ford Hall too soon. Maybe Mr. Maxwell wasn't there. Another teacher, Mr. Lauman, who lived on the first floor, came outside in his shirt-sleeves despite the temperature in the teens, following Dad. I saw Mr. Lauman say something to Dad and then point toward the Headmaster's house, a big white mansion that took up one corner of the campus, surrounded by enormous, ancient, naked elm trees. Dad began walking briskly on the cleared concrete walk toward the Headmaster's house; I met him about halfway there.

"Maxwell wasn't there," he said. "I pounded on his door and when he didn't open it, I kicked it open. I thought he was hiding, the little creep, but he wasn't there. That guy who stopped me said that Coach Hepworth is at Phillips Stevens' house and I should go over there. What's his name? Do I remember him?"

"Mr. Lauman," I answered. "You met him the last time you were up here."

"Right."

When we arrived at the Headmaster's house, Dad knocked. Mrs. Stevens opened the door and Dad introduced himself. She acted as if she was expecting both of us, although I knew she couldn't have known that we were even on the campus. "Phil is in his office over there with Arch Hepworth," she said pointing at a paneled door. "Let me tell them you're here." She left us standing in the vestibule while she went into Mr. Stevens' office. A minute later, Phillips Stevens opened the door.

"Gentlemen, come in, come in," he said heartily and warmly, but I could tell immediately that he was deeply troubled. His head was bowed and he looked very serious. Mr. Hepworth was standing behind Stevens. Dad and I went into the Headmaster's office. The walls were lined with books from floor to ceiling. The window wall looked out on the campus. I could imagine Mr. Stevens sitting in his leather chair swiveled around with his back to the desk, feet up on the windowsill, surveying his own creation. Perhaps, he would be pulling at one of his meerschaum pipes, congratulating himself for having moved the entire campus to this site fifteen years before and for having built or converted nearly all of the buildings he could see. Except for some of the old wooden houses on the edges of the campus, he had made this place virtually with his own hands. It was his whole life.

Mr. Stevens sat down in his big chair across his desk from us. "Sit down, gentlemen, sit down, please," he said, graciously indicating two chairs in front of the desk. I noticed that Mr. Hepworth wasn't there any more, although I didn't see him leave and there didn't seem to be another door.

"We've had some bad news," he began, cradling his chin in his big hands. "Mac Maxwell is dead. He took his own life late last night in a room in the Hotel Northampton. Now, Arch Hepworth has told me what you told him," he said gravely to me, as I sat paralyzed with astonishment, "so I can appreciate why you're both here. I understand that. But," he turned away from us and his voice fell, "it's over now. There isn't anything we can do about it."

Mr. Stevens stared blankly out the window at the frozen campus for several minutes while I looked first to him and then to Dad to make sense of this incomprehensible news. I couldn't tell what Dad was thinking.

After a while, Mr. Stevens turned to us. "There's been a great tragedy here," he said. "Mac Maxwell was one of the finest men I've ever known—brilliant, courageous, loyal to this school, and, perhaps, flawed, as all of us are in some way. But, whatever has happened is now over, finished and best forgotten."

"He's dead?" I cried. "Oh God, I'm so, so sorry."

"Or course you are," said Mr. Stevens, and he took a deep breath and looked at Dad sitting rigid and mute. "We're all sorry. Now, the wisest course for all of us, I think, is to say nothing about this to anyone. There would be no point. It would only drag Mac's memory through the mud and wouldn't do any of us any good at all, don't you agree?"

Dad nodded his agreement immediately. My automatic pilot took over for me and nodded my head, but all kinds of questions were bouncing around in my brain. What happened? How did it happen? How did he do it? Why did he do it? Why do all of you—Stevens, Dad, Hepworth—think he did it? Do you think it's my fault? Is that why we're not going to say anything about it—because it's my fault?

"Good," said Mr. Stevens. "I'm glad we all agree on that. Bumppo, I'll explain to everybody that you were too upset to go to the memorial service, if you don't want to go. We'll do that next Monday morning at Chapel. I'll suspend classes and all activities for that day. I've spoken to the general who was Mac's commanding officer in France during the War. He can't be here Monday but wishes he could, so he could say something about Mac. I'll talk about him, of course. I've called his mother but haven't been able to speak with her yet. She's very old and frail. I don't know yet if there are others I'll need to call but I do know that Mac didn't have any brothers or sisters and his father died before the war." Turning to me, he said, "Bumppo, I hope you can stay here and carry on. I know you can do it and I also know that would be the best thing for you to do."

"Okay," said the automatic pilot.

"Fine, then," Dad said with relief, as if he'd just settled a lawsuit or ironed out one of life's little wrinkles. He stood up and stretched his shoulders back. "I might as well get going back to New York."

And, he did—leaving me to deal with the uncomprehending tears of my schoolmates who were never told how Maxwell died or what had happened and to write Maxwell's obituary for the front page of *The Willistonian* and to weigh countless times in my own mind the heaviness of the knowledge that what had happened between me and Maxwell had directly resulted in his death and ask myself if I had killed him. And I did ask. And the answer was always "yes."

Mr. Stevens gave me a couple of sheets of paper headed "Curriculum Vita—G. McCall Maxwell" to use in writing the obituary for *The Willistonian*. I'd forgotten about the "G."—it stood for George, which Mr. Maxwell had never used. He'd done lots of things. He'd gotten two degrees, a B.A. from Yale in 1939 and an M.A. from Harvard after he left the Army in 1946. He'd taught at Lake Forest Day School, a small, private school in a posh Chicago suburb, after his graduation from Yale until he went into the Army in 1941. He'd risen to the rank of Major. He told me once that he'd been a translator for some conferences between General Eisenhower and General DeGaulle and that DeGaulle had awarded him a medal. No medals were listed on the sheet and I wondered if Mr. Maxwell had told me the truth. According to the sheet, he went back to teach at Lake Forest Day School after the war and was its Headmaster for seven years before he joined the Williston faculty in 1954.

Why had he left Lake Forest? Did they find out? Or, did he leave before they could guess? I wanted to go out there and ask questions. No, I didn't. I really didn't want to do anything except forget about him, but I couldn't do that.

Mr. Stevens told me that Mr. Maxwell's mother was too old to come from Chicago. She asked that Mac's body be shipped back to Chicago so he could be buried there. He was thirty-nine-years-old.

Mr. Stevens wanted a picture of Mr. Maxwell to run with the obituary and gave me a batch to choose from. I considered several, but finally picked the one he'd chosen himself for *The Log*, Williston's yearbook, the year before. I looked at his eyes in all those pictures—small and a little squinty behind his glasses with clear plastic frames. Was there something there I should have seen? Was there something in the tense smile on his face in every one of them that should have told me something? How could I have spent so much time with him and not figured it out? How could I really have thought he was my best friend? What about the other Favored Few—did they know? Were they doing things with him, and I just never knew it? Some of them were incredibly upset—truly flattened with grief. What about them? But, above all, why did he pick me?

Obituaries are pretty straightforward and factual, thank God, or I'd never have been able to do it, but it was still bad enough. "McCall Maxwell died suddenly…" I began, leaving out the "G." on purpose and also leaving out "AS A RESULT OF A FUCKING BULLET HE FIRED INTO HIS FUCKING BRAIN!" I did write, "Mr. Maxwell, forty years old at his death and a faggot, had taught French at Williston for the past seven years and was a favorite with the boys, or vice versa." I felt almost as if he was standing there over me editing the stupid, warped black whimsy out of the obituary, as he had done with me with hundreds of articles over the last two years, so I first crossed out "…and a faggot" and changed the rest to "…and had his favorite boys." Then I crossed that out, too.

The whole obituary went that way. I just couldn't help wondering about things such as what gun did he use? Was it his World War II revolver? Did he even have a World War II revolver? If so, why hadn't I ever seen it? Did he write a note or anything? Mr. Stevens hadn't told me about any suicide note and I didn't ask, but I wondered. I hoped he hadn't. I wasn't sure if I wanted to know, if he did. Was I in it? Did Mr. Stevens know about Mr. Maxwell? Maybe Mr. Stevens was mentioned in the note and that's why he didn't tell me. What does Mr. Stevens know? It's impossible he doesn't know something. Maybe I missed the signs, but I wasn't looking for them. It was Stevens' goddamn job to look for them. He must have known. And, Mr. Hepworth. He wasn't all that shocked when I'd told him. He just sat there calmly as he figured out what I should do. Why didn't they do something? Didn't they care? Why didn't I do something more sensible than going berserk? Maybe if I'd kept my head, Mr. Maxwell would still be alive. Yes, he'd almost surely still be alive.

I finished the damn thing on schedule and gave it to Mr. Stevens to edit. He started changing some words and adding others. "I'll take it from here," he said dismissing me.

The rest of the school year was a blur. I wrote something insipid to finish off the college applications and got them in the mail in time. They didn't seem important. Somehow, I got through my classes. I was still operating on automatic pilot, going from one class to another, then back to my room to pretend to study. I was in a funk. Even the letter from Harvard inviting me to join the Class of 1961 didn't help much. It didn't seem like such a big deal after all, at least for a few days after it came and I got a similar letter from Brown. Then it began to sink in, that some things were real after all. Fred L. Glimp was real.

I hadn't told anybody about the Harvard letter except Mr. Stevens, and, of course, Bruce and Steve. I wrote a postcard to Dad. It was to the point: "Got into Harvard. Also some other places. Not sure where I want to go." I didn't want to talk to him and I didn't want him to think that if I decided to go to Harvard, which I did right away, it was because of him. I didn't even want to think that I was doing it for him, or the family. I was going to do it because if what I thought of as the best college in the country accepted me, I'd be crazy not to go. Steve David got into Harvard, too, and so did David Montague, but Montague decided to go to MIT proving what a jerk he really was.

Mr. Hepworth went easy on me and didn't mention the times I'd miss practice. But, when I noticed that it felt good to pound the ball I stopped cutting practice. My game improved and I began to play number two singles and number one doubles. I was captain of the varsity tennis team that year and all of a sudden we were having a winning season. For some reason—it must have been a very slow news day—*The New York Times* ran my picture standing with racquet in hand next to Coach Hepworth with a story about the Williston tennis team's season and its rosy prospects. Dad saw the story and called me about it. He said a lot of his friends had seen it and had called him. He wondered why I hadn't told him about the story. I said I didn't think they'd actually print it and was surprised that they did. He said he wished I'd told him and that he felt foolish not knowing about it when his friends called. I felt great about the story and my picture and hadn't wanted to tell Dad because I was afraid he'd spoil it somehow. His call almost did that.

Aside from gaining some degree of release from thrashing tennis balls, I felt useless. I didn't have much energy and didn't seem to care about anything. Bruce and Steve thought I was broken up over Mr. Maxwell's death and I didn't say I wasn't. I didn't say anything. I started going into town to DeBarbieri's again. Helen's insane predicaments with Boris and her husband took my mind off my problems. It seemed comforting that other people had it worse.

Mr. Maxwell's rooms were locked. I wouldn't have gone back

in there for anything in the world. But, I missed him and missed going in there for coffee or to read the newspaper or watch television or just hang around. I'd lost my best friend—but maybe he wasn't my best friend.

When our yearbook, *The Log*, came out, I flipped through the front pages wondering what Phil Stevens would put in there about Mr. Maxwell. I found one page headed "In Memoriam" that was blank except for pictures of G. McCall Maxwell and Paul Elkins with heavy black borders and their dates. For Mac, it simply said:

G. McCALL MAXWELL
SEPTEMBER 21, 1917 – JANUARY 30, 1957

I guessed Stevens couldn't write anything either. But why not? He didn't kill Mr. Maxwell. I did that. At least, no one said I didn't.

I WENT THROUGH graduation like a zombie. I didn't feel anything, not good, not bad—not even when I was initiated into the Cum Laude Society, which was a very big deal to Mr. Stevens and Mr. Rouse. The night after graduation, I went with a large group of my classmates to a party in Greenwich given by the parents of "Tiger" Revson, the son of one of the founders of Revlon. Tiger had joined our class at Williston for his senior year after having been kicked out of another school, Choate, I think. His father—maybe he was looped—started trying to dance very close to some of the girlfriends of the guys who were there and the guys got a little upset about it. I didn't care. I didn't have a girlfriend, there or anywhere. Joann hadn't called or written to me after she came to Williston for the Senior Prom. She was never in when I called. Maybe I was so boring at the Prom she couldn't stand it. Maybe I did something to make her mad. It didn't seem to matter. All I could think about was why had Mr. Maxwell done it?

Chapter Nine

I WAS EXPECTING to curl up with the fog that summer—almost looking forward to its silence and familiarity. But, it wasn't there! There wasn't any fog at all for once. Dad seemed happy. At least, he took it easy on Mom, and that made her happy. But I still couldn't feel anything, so I started making my own fog—getting grouchy at Betty and Margaret, our Irish maids, and not talking much to anybody. I just brooded and goofed around the house, watched TV and went fishing with Bert Hand a few times. Even that didn't seem to help. I couldn't help asking the question over and over: Why did Mr. Maxwell kill himself. Why? I just kept asking, and no answers came. Harvard seemed an eon away. Then, something good happened.

Since I was going to Harvard in the fall and now Dad thought I had a future, he said he thought I should have a reward and some R&R because of what had happened with "that teacher." He also thought Bob needed a lift, although why he thought so about Bob wasn't clear. I knew that Bob was still wondering what to do with the rest of his life now that he'd graduated from Harvard —he'd been working as an intern at IBM and was thinking of going to Oxford or Cambridge for a while, or maybe law school, or maybe something else would come up—but Dad was never around, so what could he know? Anyhow, Dad came up with the amazing idea that Bob and I should drive the sporty blue and white Dodge that replaced Mom's Rambler out to Banff in the Canadian Rockies and he and Mom would take the train and meet us there. We'd all stay at the Banff Springs Hotel for a few days and then go up to the Chateau Lake Louise for a few more days. Then they'd go back home on the train and Bob and I could go on in the car to California and drive back across the country. Take a friend to share the driving, he suggested to Bob.

How great that sounded after I'd been thinking I'd have to spend the summer selling something door-to-door, killing yew trees or just moping around in the fog. Before Dad came up with the idea of the trip out West, I thought about going back to the tree nursery in disguise and finishing the job—I'd kill all the frigging baby yew trees and then disappear stealthily into the night. But, with the trip, I wouldn't have to do anything like that this summer.

In no time, Bob had lined up my old nemesis Lang Stevenson to go with us and we were off, going straight out to the Badlands of South Dakota almost without stopping. We continued west through Wyoming to Yellowstone Park and then went north through Glacier Park to Calgary and up to Banff. Meeting Mom and Dad there didn't seem too unreasonable, and we ate a lot

better with them around. Lang chased a tall, leggy Texas girl
with, so he said, a very good result. Bob and I weren't so sure
about that. We trekked around Lake Louise and rode horses up
by the glacier high above the lake until our butts were sore. It
was a good time, though, and I was too worn out most of the
time to care how much Mom drank or what Dad said or if Lang
really made it with the Texan.

After a week, we all went to the Canadian Pacific station in
Calgary, saw Mom and Dad off on a train to Toronto and put
the car and ourselves on a train to Vancouver that went along
the deep and rugged and wildly beautiful Fraser River canyon.
From Vancouver, we drove down the coast heading toward San
Francisco, with a detour to drop in on Lynn (for Llewellyn)
Jones, the ripe and lively daughter of John Jones, my eighth grade
Sunday school teacher at St. Barnabas Church in Irvington. Lynn
spent summers at her grandmother's house in Crystal Bay on
Lake Tahoe, near the California-Nevada border. She'd actually
asked me to drop by if we were near enough, but probably didn't
think we were really going to do it. However, sad to say, Bob
and Lang weren't interested in my love life, which was withering
badly since Joann hadn't spoken to me in months. Since Lang's
claimed fornication with the tall Texan he'd met at Banff, all he
wanted to do was follow her to some place in Texas we couldn't
find on the map. Bob was on the fence. He was interested in seeing Lake Tahoe but wasn't so sure that staying with my "little"
girl friend was the way to do it, but he wasn't too excited about
chasing all over Texas for Lang's big girl either.

I finally won, but at great cost. I had to promise Bob and
Lang that I would not insist on hearing Debbie Reynolds sing

"Tammy" one more time for the entire rest of the trip, a harsh penalty. On the way to Lake Tahoe, we stopped for a night at the Timberline Lodge on Mount Hood in Oregon, I fell deeply in love with a folk singer named Molly Scott who was singing and playing her guitar in the bar there. She was so beautiful, the place was so beautiful with snow in the summer and a big roaring fire in the giant stone fireplace, and the cozy, rustic bar and the folk songs she sang were so wonderful, I almost didn't feel I was being unfaithful to Joann, who probably was dating somebody else and could care less, or Lynn, who probably had a boyfriend at Lake Tahoe for all I knew.

While I was listening to Molly, I realized that I hadn't thought of McCall Maxwell or Chilson Leonard for hours—maybe even a whole day. I could have stayed at Timberline forever, but Molly probably would have gotten sick of a kid like me hanging around all the time, so I got over my crush with great pain and Bob and Lang dragged me off to get back on the road—next stop: Lake Tahoe.

We finally got to the Jones family's "camp"—we should all have to go to camp in such places—on Crystal Bay, aptly named because you could see the bottom clear as a bell even at about a hundred feet. Yes, there were a bunch of cabins and a main lodge, but it wasn't like any camp I'd ever seen before. Each cabin was a neat little log house with two or three bedrooms, a living room and a kitchen. We got one of the bigger cabins.

Lynn wasn't "little" in any sense of the word and was truly gorgeous and so was everything else. Lang—randy Lang—fell hard for Lynn. It was disgusting how he changed and all of a sudden got great manners and began helping out with the dishes and other chores and being so nice—just while Lynn was around, of course. When she wasn't, he reverted to his usual character, which was generally mean and slovenly. I seriously considered telling Lynn about Texas but, remembering how he almost killed me once, I didn't.

Lang's falling for Lynn put a crimp in my romantic plans, for sure. Lynn liked all the attention Lang gave her and flirted with him so much it turned my stomach. What could I do? Get out of there as soon as possible, that's what.

I suggested we leave a couple of days early. Now it was Lang who wanted to stay but even his offer to restore my full "Tammy" rights didn't sway me. Since Bob was again on the fence but decided, after about two minutes thinking about it, that he didn't like watching Lang and Lynn fool around any more than I did, Lang was outvoted and we left Lake Tahoe.

On to San Francisco, to Fisherman's Wharf, the Purple Onion and the Kingston Trio at the hungry i. We drank lots of beer—I got served everywhere without even showing my bogus Massachusetts driver's license—and almost got into lots of trouble at a "pad"—one entire floor of a huge warehouse in North Beach, which was a pretty shabby part of town, inhabited by about three people per square foot and led by someone named "Big Daddy," a huge, ragged, bearded guy who smelled of something strange and looked like Bigfoot. While we didn't think we were square before we went there, we did after that. I had actually never heard of "pot" before, and declined to smoke it in favor of my beloved Chesterfields—something that nobody in Big Daddy's pad could understand. They thought that smoking cigarettes was unhealthy and not cool, but smoking pot was just fine, and they were all doing a lot of it. As well as drinking lots of awful wine from a communal wineskin.

Dad had asked us, when we got to San Francisco, to stop by and see his old college suite mate Bob Bullard, which we did, although we didn't really want to. While we were sitting in their living room with Mrs. Bullard, her husband popped in to shake hands and slap us on the back. What a pleasure to see us, he said. He was a genial fellow who'd done pretty well in the past 30-odd years, judging from all of the art and other stuff that was all over the huge living room. Mr. Bullard started to reminisce, which is why we didn't particularly want to meet him—we were certain to hear a lot of stories about the Old Days at Harvard.

Had Dad told us the one about the day Mr. Bullard and Dad's other roommates filled up a bathtub to make gin for a party that night and then went out for classes and left the alcohol and juniper to age? No, Bob said, but Mr. Bullard was going on anyway. He said Dad had gone into the bathroom in the empty suite and found the bathtub already full, so he climbed in and was taking a bath in the alcohol when the other guys came back. They yelled and screamed at him for being so dumb and cancelled the party. Dad was supposed to have waited until the dirt settled and then he drank a lot of it. Sure, I thought. I could just hear him whining that it didn't really happen that way. I didn't believe it, anyhow. It didn't fit. Mr. Bullard left to go to a lunch appointment after telling us that story, swearing it was true. As he was leaving, a blonde goddess appeared and gave him a kiss as he was putting his hat on. "Have a good lunch, Daddy," said the goddess. Mrs. Bullard took her by the elbow and steered her over to Bob, Lang and me. "This is my daughter, Ruth" I think she said. "She has an identical twin named Ellen, who isn't here right now. I say 'identical twin' although that's not exactly right. They do look alike, but the other one has much prettier cheekbones. See how Ruth's are flat and give her face such a drawn and tense look?" Mrs. Bullard pinched Ruth's cheek and tugged her face towards us to show us the flaw. "Ellen's eyes are also much prettier—a much deeper, electric blue, not washed out like Ruth's." I looked at the carpet, rich, deep and a sort of light, washed-out blue. I didn't want to look at Ruth. How had she survived this long— she was, maybe, eighteen? Are all parents insane?

We hit the trail again, down through Cypress Point, Monterey and Big Sur to Los Angeles, which wasn't too much fun—a guy I later was told was Nicky Hilton, Elizabeth Taylor's former husband who was still a local celebrity then even though he'd been divorced from her for years, staggered blind drunk into the men's room of a bar on the Sunset strip where I was taking a pee, lurched to the urinal next to me and pissed on my shoe. That was Los Angeles for me. Then, off to Las Vegas.

I loved Vegas. We stayed up all night, slept all day and saw Patience and Prudence at one hotel and *The Pajama Game* at another, gorging on the endless free food. No one asked me how old I was and I played roulette until the sun came up. I even won, although I had some help from a croupier who looked like he wasn't much older than I was. I was the only person at a table at about three in the morning and the croupier watched me for about an hour losing on number 14, which was Gil Hodges' number. He told me to bet number 26 because he'd been there for hours and seen 26 come up a lot. He thought the wheel was slightly off balance and they'd fix it sometime but until they did, he told me to go for it. So, I gave up thinking that Gil Hodges was going to bring me luck and started betting a single sliver dollar on number 26. It gave me some qualms when I remembered the 26 I got on my *Scarlet Letter* essay for Chilson Leonard, but maybe my luck had turned. I had some bad moments at first when I lost, thinking the guy had conned me, but then I began to win. By about five in the morning, I was up over five hundred dollars, which was what Dad had given both Bob and me when we started.

Just as I was thinking how impossible it would be to keep my winnings a secret from Bob and Lang, who were sure to spend them for me if and when they found out, I heard a woman begin to shout and yell about something at one of the long bars. I looked over and saw Bob, ducking and weaving, with his arms up to protect his head, as the woman pummeled him with her purse and screamed at him. Wow! I didn't want to cash in my chips and leave my lucky spot at the roulette table, but he was my brother, after all. So, I asked my friend the croupier to keep my seat warm while I went to see what was happening. Bob was retreating in the face of the furious onslaught. As I got there, she gave Bob one last whack with her purse and shouted "fucking cheapskate" as she marched off leaving Bob leaning against a bar stool with his mouth open in amazement.

"What in hell was that all about," I naturally asked him. He didn't seem like he wanted to talk about it a lot, but he had to tell me something. So, he said that she and he had a difference of opinion on what the value of her services might be. Bob had offered her twenty-five dollars to do the deed and she wanted a hundred. Bob had come up to fifty, max, and refused to budge—

which was a good thing because all he had was about fifty bucks —and she got furious and began to bop him. That did add a new dimension for me to Bob; I didn't think he'd ever done the deed before either and, if this episode was any indication of how he got along with women, he might be a virgin for a long time. Anyhow, I watched the woman, who I now saw was a really good-looking girl, prowl around the room after bigger game. I'd never seen someone I knew was a prostitute before and I must admit that thinking about doing it with her got me pretty excited. And, I had the money.

I don't know if I chickened out or what, but I didn't do it. So, Bob didn't get laid that night and neither did I. However, I did win over five hundred dollars. Since all Bob had left was the fifty dollars he'd offered the girl and I was rich, he was pretty nice to me—I even got to listen to "Tammy" a couple of times while I was driving and Bob and Lang held their ears. I paid for a lot more than my share of our meals from then on, but I was pretty sure Gil Hodges would have been a good guy and done that, too, since it seemed the right thing under the circumstances.

We drove on to the Grand Canyon, got out of the car for at least a minute and looked over the rim down to the Colorado River far below, said "Wow!" a couple of times and moved on.

We'd used up most of the summer and so we made a beeline for home—Lang had to get ready to go back to Princeton for his senior year and I was about to enroll as a freshman at Harvard College! Bob was still wondering how to postpone real life. The rest of the trip home was a blur of driving straight through the heart of the country to the New York Thruway at Buffalo, which took us all the way back to Ardsley.

The best part of the whole adventure was that I began to feel fresh—as if I had a few broken bones somewhere in my body that were slowly but steadily mending. I had almost stopped thinking about Chilson Leonard and McCall Maxwell. During the day, when it was my turn to drive and Bob and Lang were sleeping, I couldn't help going over the whole scene with Mr. Maxwell in my mind, over and over again. I'd remember details: the grain of the wood on the bookshelves that lined the passageway to Mr. Maxwell's room, a blue striped button-down shirt crumpled up on Mr. Maxwell's bed, small gold-framed pictures of somebody on the tall chest Mr. Maxwell was leaning on when I got to the end of the passageway, and, always, the sound of his voice saying he loved me. At night, I would dream so often about it, or about Chilson Leonard torturing me in some far-off jungle, that I hated to go to sleep and looked for any reason to stay up later and later until I was so exhausted I'd fall asleep and not dream about anything.

AT THE DINNER table the first night we were home, Dad asked about the trip. Bob took him from Banff to San Francisco and then I jumped in, not wanting Bob to get us onto the slippery slope of all the bars we went to. I said we'd gone to see the Bullards at their house, and had a good time.

"Mrs. Bullard was a little strange about one of her daughters," I said, leaving out the details, "but Mr. Bullard seemed happy to see us and talk about the old days with you at Harvard. He told us the story about you and the bathtub gin."

"What gin?" he asked suspiciously. "I don't remember any gin story."

"Well," I continued, knowing that I was on thin ice, "he said you came back to your room one day when nobody else was there and found the bathtub full, so you climbed in. Only it wasn't water, it was gin. The others freaked out and called off the party, but you were supposed to have drunk it. He thought it was pretty funny." I left out the part about the dirt settling.

"That's ridiculous," he said. "It never, ever happened! And I don't want to hear another thing from either of you about it—understand? So that was your trip, huh? I'll bet you had a lot of laughs on me about that, but it never happened, so the laughs are on you." He got up from the table and threw his napkin down. "I just can't believe that I gave you this wonderful trip and all you come back with is a cock-and-bull story about me! What a waste! I'm terribly disappointed in both of you," he said as he stalked out of the dining room and clomped loudly upstairs and slammed the door to the bedroom. Mom watched him go up in her usual haze. After we heard the bedroom door slam shut, she turned to us with a frown and said she wondered what that was all about. We both said we didn't know.

"Have I told you what's going on with the animals?" Mom asked us earnestly.

"What animals?" Bob asked.

"The animals in the shelters, of course, silly." She was droopy-eyed and bleary and we didn't have a clue what she was talking about. As we helped her get through the story, it seemed that a rival animal shelter had opened up almost next door in competition with the animal shelter in Elmsford she'd been involved with for years. "It's horrible," she said with a stricken look. "It's dog eat dog!"

I couldn't wait to get out of the house and talk to someone else. Dr. Kertess. I drove up to the Kertess' house and let myself in after I heard Mrs. Kertess call to me and say something that sounded like Dr. Kertess was in the living room. I was looking forward to curling up in one of those huge chairs and letting their wings wrap themselves around me. I'd just stay there forever. What was I going to tell him? That nothing changes— my house is a looney bin? Boring. The trip out West? Probably. About Harvard? For sure. That will make him very happy. About Maxwell? Even the thought of telling another person anything about Maxwell made me feel a hot, slashing pain in my stomach. What could Dr. Kertess possibly say? What would he think? He'd come to the same conclusion I did: If I hadn't been such a wimp and gone running off in tears to Mr. Hepworth, Maxwell would still be alive. I was responsible. Simple as that. There was no other way to see it. Would it affect how he felt about me? Sure. It would have to. He'd know he misjudged me. Also, he'd probably think that, maybe I'm queer. Why else would Maxwell have picked me? Dr. Kertess wouldn't have to say anything about that, but how could he help thinking it? Why did I drop in to see him? I'll make it short and leave in a few minutes—not enough time to talk about anything much. Maybe Dr. Kertess is right—I do "tink too much."

"Zo, Bumppo," said Dr. Kertess as he went toward his favorite chair, "you've had a big trip and now you're going to Harvard. Vhat you tink about Harvard? Are you nervous?"

"A little, I guess," I answered. "I am looking forward to seeing my old Exeter pals and the expressions on their faces when they see me. Most of them don't know I'm going."

"You vant to restore your reputation, iss dat it?"

"Sure. What's wrong with that?"

"Noting, but vhat are you going to tell dem?"

"I dunno. I guess I better think that through."

"Ya, dat would be good. You know vhat I tink?" he asked and without waiting for my answer continued "I tink you vill tell dem some ting harmless and you vill not vant to get into de whole business vith some crazy teacher."

"Why do you think so?" I asked.

"Because, vhen you tink about it, you vill understand vhat dey tink iss not important. Vhat's important is vhat you tink. And, I believe you finally understand you did not deserve de treatment you got from vhats-his-name—"

"Chilson Leonard..."

"Ya, Leonard—and vhat he did to you made you tink you are stupid and vorthless, but dat isn't so. You are stronger than he is. You are also smarter than him and he is the vorthless one—dangerous, ya, but vorthless."

"I do think I'm over it—getting into Harvard sure helped. Maybe I won't tell all my old buddies the whole story. I really don't know what I'll do."

"Okay, enough. Now let's talk about some ting good. How about ve plan your trip to Europe next summer, starting vith vhen you will come see me at the Park Hotel in Frankfurt vhere I alvays stay."

Chapter Ten

HARVARD! HARVARD! EVERY day of my first weeks and months at Harvard were astonishing to me, from my first day when I registered as a member of the Class of 1961 at a huge, ancient and creepy Victorian thing known as Memorial Hall—like something out of *Great Expectations*—to the courses, all of which I found extremely interesting and for which I dutifully did all my work. Maybe I'd learned something at Williston.

As September became October and then November, and I got used to my three roommates and the daily routine of going to classes and Lamont Library to study, I fell in love with Harvard Yard. The Yard in the fall is a quiet, beautiful, special place, full of spirits. The earliest buildings, mostly built during the nineteenth century, form an inner group, and the more recent ones tend to be located on the outer perimeter near the tall iron fence that surrounds the Yard. It was much larger than I'd imagined or remembered from the time I'd spent a weekend with Bob when I was at Exeter. In fact, it was huge, big enough to hold the mammoth Widener Library, lots of old stone and brick dorms of different vintages, another big, newer library, Lamont, still another library, Houghton, for rare books, several old, ivied classroom and administrative buildings and a church, Memorial Church, which didn't look scrunched in at all. They all seemed to go together somehow, even if their ages and styles or architecture were different.

Fall, of course, meant football, even in the Ivy League. Football was only a medium big deal at Harvard, and most of the other colleges in the Ivy League, except, maybe, Cornell, which was suspected of recruiting ringers with money and perks like they did in the Big Ten. Larry Fraser, my jock roommate at Exeter, had gone from an amazing career at Exeter to Cornell on a football scholarship, but that seemed okay since he was smart—not studious, but smart. He'd gotten decent grades at Exeter somehow, and needed all the financial help he could get. Giving Larry, who was now about six feet four, weighed well over two hundred and twenty pounds and could run like a deer and catch impossible passes, a football scholarship was simply a brilliant idea for Cornell and good for Larry. Larry was no ringer. Harvard missed the boat. I hoped to see Larry sometime when Cornell played Harvard, but that game was at Cornell this year.

While football wasn't a big deal, football weekends in Cambridge were. The Saturday home games at Soldiers Field stadium across the Charles River from the Yard were the focus of lots of pre-game lunches, post-game drinks and victory parties (whether Harvard won or not) throughout the entire university.

The biggest weekend was the Yale game—The Game—if it was in Cambridge that year. Every other year, when The Game was in New Haven, the Princeton game was the biggest weekend, no matter how good or bad the teams were. This year, The Game was in New Haven, so in late October, the Harvard community boarded up its windows, hid its virgins in cellars and otherwise prepared for the two-day assault of the Green Horde from Hanover, a force of seemingly thousands of thirsty, hairy, deprived and horny animals who came to Cambridge like barbarians sacking Rome and left the infirmary full, the local bartenders exhausted and the streets dotted with puddles of puke. They were really gross. In fact, the degree of their lack of couth passed even the understanding of their Harvard peers, who weren't so long on couth themselves.

THE WEEK BEFORE the Dartmouth game arrived and I still had no date and no prospects since my supposed girlfriend, Joann, who was now at Bradford Junior College in Haverhill, had just stopped talking to me out of the blue one day earlier in the fall, just as it was becoming about impossible for her to protect her celestial chest from me any longer. Her roommate at Bradford called to tell me that she was going out with a senior at Dartmouth and didn't want to see me again. That hurt. To think of Joann with a Dartmouth guy—a barbarian!—was agony. I pretended it didn't matter that much, but it did. So, I called Betsey Thorndike, a girl from Ardsley, for whom I felt no romantic impulses at all but who was rather spectacularly beautiful. She'd be a great date for the weekend. Betsey was enthusiastic, and could stay at her sister Annie Cover's place, but said her mother wouldn't let her go unless she could bring a friend—could I fix up her friend? Whose the friend, I asked? Jewelle Wooten. You know her brother Jim-Jim from Hackley, she answered. My heart fell. Jim-Jim had two "Jims" because one wasn't enough for a person of his girth. His sister, therefore, had to be hugely fat and was undoubtedly ugly. How was I going to work this out? Somehow, I was able to get Tommy Thompson, a Harvard sophomore from Ardsley, to take a chance on Jim-Jim's sister, but only if I paid for the football tickets, the drinks, dinner, the works. In for a penny, I thought, and so Tommy and I picked up two of the most beautiful creatures on earth at South Station that Saturday morning. Jewelle turned out to be the girl I'd ogled when I'd taken foreign kids around Manhattan as a volunteer with the American Field Service the summer before my senior year at Williston. Amazingly, she was also the girl that Dr. Kertess talked to, just like he talked to me. Wow, I thought. If Dr. Kertess likes her, she must be pretty special. When Tommy and I went to pick up Betsey and Jewelle for the dance that night, Annie's husband, Mac Cover, took one look and drooled, calling Jewelle "a stunning mass of undulating femininity in yellow." I just thought she was the best thing I'd ever seen in any color. We had a wonderful time at the game and the parties afterwards and I made it clear, I think, to Jewelle that I wanted to see her again.

A COUPLE OF weeks later, I was facing another dateless Saturday. But, I didn't want to go to another Harvard football game and freeze to death. I knew it was the day of the big game between Exeter and Andover, its chief rival for nearly a hundred years.

I didn't know what I wanted to do, but I never considered going to up to Exeter. I hadn't been back to Exeter since I'd left a lifetime before. I'd even stopped thinking about going back and tying Chilson Leonard to a chair while I tortured him slowly to death. In fact, I'd pretty much decided that I would never go back. Exeter had become a receding memory, like those old sepia photographs of Mom I didn't care to dust off and look at anymore, probably because, also like Mom, I wasn't sure of what had happened to her. But, the Thursday before that weekend, all that changed.

My big lecture course in Humanities—"Hum Two"—ended oddly that day. Our teacher, the famous eccentric Professor John Finley, who could remember the names of almost all of the thousands of new and former students who lived in Eliot House, where he reigned, but often forgot where he was standing, had become totally enraptured with his own description of Penelope's ineffable, bittersweet joy upon finally seeing her beloved husband Odysseus, home alive at last, ten years after the end of the Trojan War. As he spoke, Professor Finley paraded theatrically around the stage of Sanders Theater, the large Victorian amphitheater in Memorial Hall where the lecture was held each week. The stage was flanked by two huge marble statues on pedestals of American patriots whose names I never learned. The statue on the left as you look at the stage was of an orator in flowing robes declaiming, probably on the glories of independence.

Peter Bradford, my old Exeter pal, also now at Harvard, was sitting next to me and predicted what was going to happen. He'd heard that sometimes Professor Finley would hop on one of the pedestals—pretty neat hop—enthralled with whatever he was lecturing about. But, the Professor had a problem. He'd be up there clutching one of the statutes but didn't want to jump down and risk breaking a leg. He had to have help getting down. Peter hoped that he'd have a go at it that day and watched with mounting glee as the Professor moved closer and closer to the edge of the stage near the sculpture on the left side.

"Bumppo, watch him! He's going to do it, I know it! Just watch! By the way, are you going up to the Andover game? It's on Saturday."

"No. I haven't thought about it," I said untruthfully. "Are you? How come you know he's going to do it? And, if he does, what makes you think he'll get stuck up there? Pretty unlikely, I'd say. And pretty ridiculous, if he does," I whispered.

"I think he does it every year. Maybe, it's some kind of weird challenge for him. If he gets back to the stage, we're all supposed to clap—he expects it! If he doesn't, we're not supposed to notice and just leave. Why don't you go to the Andover game this year? It's been a couple of years since you've been up there. It'll be good for you to go back. A lot of guys you know will probably be there. C'mon."

"I'm not sure. I think I really want to get a date for the Princeton game."

"C'mon, asshole. Do you good. It's too late to get a date now, anyway. There goes Finley! And, you can give someone a ride – like me. I need a ride."

"Okay, I'll think about it."

"Don't think about it, just say you'll do it! Hey, Bumppo, lookit that—Finley's got his hand on the statue! Do you good to see the old place again, you know, exorcise the ghosts."

I began to think that, maybe, it would be good to see the old place again, especially Mrs. Baker. I missed her. Maybe I really could put it behind me and stop thinking so much about Exeter and Chilson Leonard and what had happened. Would Mr. Leonard remember? How could he forget? Was it possible that what he did to me was nothing more to him that crushing a bug? No, I couldn't believe that. But, if I saw him again—and he always went to football games—maybe, if he knew that I'd gotten into Harvard, he would see that he'd been wrong about me. He probably wouldn't be able to say so but, maybe, I'd see something in his eyes that would tell me "Kid, I went a bit overboard, I guess. I'm sorry I screwed up your entire life, or tried my best to. I must have gone bonkers. I have decided to dedicate my remaining years to intensive psychiatric therapy with Dr. Heyl, who has agreed to take me on despite the difficulty of my case. I hope someday, somehow, you'll be able to forgive me." I saw him falling to his knees, head bowed, at my feet. "Of course I forgive you, Mr. Leonard. You were a crazy, sadistic person, cruel and obsessed. I accept your plea of insanity and absolve you of any guilt whatever. After all, I got into Harvard! You didn't kill me. You just tried!"

"Bumppo, look there! He's going to get up on the pedestal—I'm sure of it!"

It did look that way. The Professor was looking up, eyeing the statue as if he was a bout to spring at it.

"Okay, Bradford, maybe I'll do it. What time do you want to leave?"

"Is about eleven okay?"

"Sure. Meet me in front of Hayes-Bickford's at about eleven?"

"Deal," he said, pleased that he'd been able to cajole me into going back. He wanted me to like Exeter for some reason. I felt a little bit like Professor Finley, like I was about to jump somewhere I didn't want to be.

I met Peter at Hayes-Bickford's, a grungy coffee shop in Harvard Square where the manager cashed my checks thinking, wrongly, I was the son of the owner. It was brilliantly sunny, clear and cold. Mist was rising off the black water of the Charles River in the morning sunshine. Bradford got in the front seat of my excellent black and white Ford.

We drove north from Cambridge and got to Exeter before one o'clock, so I passed by the art gallery to see if Mrs. Baker was there, but she'd already left for lunch and the game. I knew she'd be at the game because she went to everything. It felt pretty good to be back. Nothing had changed; everything was where it used to be. I wondered if any of the kids there had discovered the Eagle's Nest. I wondered if Leonard was torturing someone else.

I parked the car in a parking lot in a field near the stadium and Bradford and I walked to the stadium together without saying anything. It was about a half-hour or less before the kickoff, and the stands were just beginning to fill up. I ambled around a bit on the cinder track that bordered the grass of the field while Peter stopped to talk with a teacher I didn't know. Somehow, I lost track of him for a moment but looked around and saw Bradford waving to friends and slapping backs. I heard kids come up to Peter saying, "Hey, man, how the hell are you?" so often it was making me sick. There must be something better to say when you meet someone you haven't seen in a while. It was getting to me, kids racing over and jumping on him and yelling, "I don't believe it! Bradford!" as if it was the biggest surprise in the world to see Peter there. But, Peter didn't seem to mind. He looked down at the cinder track a lot and smiled a sort of humble smile that didn't look all that sincere to me. But even Peter must have gotten sick of saying, "Yeah, Harvard's really great! You've gotta sneak out and come down and see what it's all about!" I think he must have said that a hundred times, sometimes even to guys he wouldn't have let through the door if they'd actually shown up. A lot of kids seemed to like Bradford. Even a few teachers came up to him to shake hands and say hello. That was good to see—a quiet guy who was liked so much, like Gil Hodges. It also made me feel good that a few guys remembered me, too.

Most of the really good friends I'd made in the past few months at Harvard—except Bradford, of course—hadn't gone to Exeter and so weren't at the Andover game. Larry was playing for Cornell that day. Seth Bingham was at Yale and Booger was at Georgetown. I didn't know where my other buddies had gone to college, but I didn't see any of them milling around the track. But still, I did recognize a lot of faces, since the seniors now had been Preps my last year there, but I wasn't terrific at remembering names. "Hey there fella! How ya doin'?" with a "Hi Pal" now and then for variety got me through the greeting stage pretty well. After that, I found that they all wanted to know what had really happened to me three years ago. Exeter's amazing legend factory had apparently been working overtime on my story. One kid asked if it was true that I'd become a professional gambler since I got caught running the roulette wheel in Wentworth Hall. Most everyone seemed a little disappointed that I was at

Harvard now, back in the boring mainstream, and without some amazing story of exotic shenanigans.

I saw Mrs. Baker up in the stands and tried to catch her eye. I knew that my being there would probably make her worry about Mr. Leonard and me. Would I cause some awful incident—maybe attack Mr. Leonard? Would she have to help me out? She'd told Dad that Mr. Leonard was the vengeful type who would get back at her somehow if she did anything to help, maybe get her fired, and she couldn't afford that. I remembered Dad telling her that she owed him something and should try to help me, but I thought she was right—Mr. Leonard was too much for her to take on. Anyhow, I wasn't planning to cause an incident. I really hoped Mr. Leonard wouldn't be there or, if he was, that we wouldn't come across each other.

Mrs. Baker was wearing a white ski parka with a fur collar and had a red and white Exeter scarf wrapped around her neck—there were dozens of those scarves in the stands around her—and a red blanket around her shoulders. She'd brought a cushion to sit on. I wished I'd thought to do that. The concrete seats in the stadium could get pretty cold. I went over to where she was getting ready to sit down.

"Hi, Mrs. Baker!" I said with some real enthusiasm, because it was good to see a friendly face up there. I looked in her eyes, but there wasn't the old sparkle there. She looked a little pinched. After an awkward pause when I was trying to figure out something else to say, Mrs. Baker said I should come back to her house after the game for something warm. Sounds great, I said. I began to leave, when Mrs. Baker clutched my arm.

"Bumppo, I haven't seen Chilson, but he's bound to be here. Be careful," she said with real concern.

"Do you think he still remembers me, or that he still gives a damn about me?" I asked her, really wishing she could actually give me the answer.

"I don't know," she said, "but something tells me that you should watch out for him and stay out of his way—for your own sake."

I said okay, I'd try to stay out of his way and went back down to the track to find Bradford. I searched the clusters of people on the track for a few moments but couldn't find him. I looked up at Mrs. Baker sitting in the stands, her hair shimmering white in the thin early afternoon sun, like a halo. She looked worried and I knew she had to be freezing. She looked down from the stands, scanning the crowd as the stadium was slowly filling up. Then our eyes met and she kind of winced and her hands jerked up a bit. She looked away from me, her eyes suddenly shifting from mine to something in back of me. She seemed to be looking past me somewhere and then she waved or pointed to someone behind me. I turned around to see who it was. But, I didn't see anybody I recognized.

Probably some friend of hers—hope it wasn't Mr. Leonard, I thought. She hadn't seemed overjoyed to see me. I knew she was my friend, but I guess I had to accept that the way I'd left had been pretty tough on her, too, with Dad all over her trying to get her to do something she couldn't. I was worried about what she said when she warned me about Mr. Leonard. Maybe, it hadn't been a great idea to come. I was looking at my feet with my hands in my pockets, shuffling along with the crowd moving toward the stands, thinking depressing thoughts and kicking lumps of cinders now and then, when I bumped straight into something solid. I realized that I'd jostled a large person because I wasn't watching out where I was going, so I looked up to apologize—straight into the acid-etched face of Chilson Leonard.

"Excuse me, Mr. Leonard," I said. "I didn't mean to barge into you like that, I just wasn't looking."

"You didn't. I wanted to see if it was really you."

I didn't understand what he'd meant until later, so I just smiled a little nervously. "Yup, it's me alright. I wondered if you'd remember me. I'm at Harvard now. I wanted to say hello to you again."

That's all I said, and I put my hand out to shake hands with him not knowing what else to do. He looked at my hand in a strange way.

"You're at Harvard?" he asked, his voice rising.

"Yes, sir. I really like it a lot."

He was still looking at my hand, which I'd been holding out there while he examined it, his eyes closing to little slits in the deep creases of his face. We stayed that way for a moment, a frozen tableau.

Suddenly Mr. Leonard moved. I heard him make a guttural noise as he bent closer to my hand and spat on it. With his huge right arm, he wiped me out of his way, stomping straight ahead through the place where I was standing and headed for the portals leading out of the stadium. I watched him go. He didn't look back.

I looked at my hand—it was still out there waiting for Mr. Leonard to shake it. How odd, I thought, to see Mr. Leonard's spit there; it was a big gob, sort of foamy with little bubbles.

Would it freeze? I was shivering. My mind was blank. I stood there looking at my hand. After a while, I walked to the edge of the cinder track and wiped my hand on the grass of the field. Then, I went to my seat where Bradford was waiting. He didn't say anything and was eager for the kickoff, so I was sure that he hadn't seen what happened. I didn't tell him.

I felt tired. My arms became heavy; they seemed to weigh a thousand pounds and I couldn't lift them. My hands wouldn't work and my legs felt stiff. Got to drive back. Drive? Drive for, maybe, two hours with the traffic? I didn't think I could do that. But, to be back in Cambridge, at Harvard, lying on my own bed in my own room in Lionel B-12, yes, I wanted that. Tell Bradford I want to get out of here. But Bradford doesn't drive, goddamn City kid, and I don't think I can do it. My arms weigh a thousand pounds and my hands don't work.

What just happened, I asked myself? But, I couldn't think. I ached. I wanted to feel better. I wanted to be somewhere all alone. Did I want to turn on the oven? I wanted to leave Exeter forever—right now!

Should I run after Mr. Leonard and punch him in the frigging face! Kick him in the balls? Stomp him! That's what I should do. But I'm not going to do that, am I? Maybe I imagined it? I should just leave. But, why? Where's Mr. Leonard? He's gone. Mr. Leonard's gone! You're here. Mrs. Baker's here. Bradford's here. You have friends here. Mr. Leonard has no friends. Don't leave. Mr. Leonard's gone. He can't do anything more to you. And, what did he do? Spit on your hand? Pathetic!

Bradford sensed something was wrong. "Are you okay, Bumppo? You don't want to go, do you?"

"Go?" I answered. "Why should we do that? We just got here and The Game's about to start. What's the matter with you, Bradford, you wimp?"

Peter's look of concern changed and he broke into a huge, wide, happy grin. My arms didn't weigh a thousand pounds anymore. They felt as light as feathers and my legs were strong. My hands worked and my arms surged with miraculous strength. I had never felt so powerful, or peaceful, in my life.

"Right, Bumppo. Goddamn right!" he said as we heard the whistle blow and everyone stood up to see Exeter kick off to Andover. I looked around after the Andover player was buried under a pile of red uniforms inside his own ten yard line. I saw Mrs. Baker. She was looking at me too, but this time she didn't look away. She had a tight little smile on her face like she was all choked up or something. I thought I should do something after I'd been looking right in her eye for a while, so I smiled and waved at her, giving her a thumb's up. Then Mrs. Baker did the most amazing thing. She kept on standing after everyone else sat down. She started clapping. She was standing there, halfway up the stands, looking at me with a big smile and clapping her mittened hands way out in front of her, like a trained seal. People looked at her as if she'd gone bonkers.

Smiling? Clapping? Whoa, I thought, wait a minute. She's right! What Mr. Leonard did was so strange and excessive that he must be nuts! How could I possibly have been the reason for the rage that was consuming him? Not likely. It must be something inside him driving him crazy. Maybe, I was just the unlucky spark, maybe just one of many that set him off. Same for Mr. Maxwell. Whatever the real reasons for Mr. Leonard's rage and Mr. Maxwell's despair, they weren't me. However terrible it was for Mr. Leonard to spend his life in angry bitterness and however tragic it was for Mr. Maxwell to end his life in an emotional hurricane, whatever devils beset them existed apart from me. They had existed before me and probably had little, if anything, to do with me. Maybe, I would never know what those reasons were, but, suddenly, that was okay. Maybe, there would be many times that people would do things for reasons of their own that I could not possibly fully understand, but that too was okay. I could live with that.

I looked up at Mrs. Baker, smiling and clapping like a seal, and smiled and waved back. I was okay. The world would go on.

And then my life began.

Epilogue

IN THE FALL of 1988, my wonderful wife, Jewelle, was asked
to speak at the twenty-fifth reunion of her class at her college
in Virginia. In helping her plan her talk, we reminisced about
the years since she'd been in college. Naturally, I also began to
ruminate on my life since I graduated from Harvard in 1961.
Something about those old memories nagged at me. Had I
ever told Jewelle about what had happened to me at Exeter and
Williston? How could I not have told her? We'd been married
then for over twenty-six years! I must have. Maybe, I did, but just
didn't remember. So, I asked her. Unbelievably, she said no, and
asked what I was talking about. I stammered and said I didn't
know where to begin.

"Since you write so well, maybe you could write about it while
I'm at my reunion this weekend," she said. "Then I'll read whatever you write when I get back."

That sounded fine to me and we left it that way.

As that week progressed, the memories began to swirl in my mind. I went back in time and actually re-lived some of those horrible days. I could see the butt rooms at Exeter, Principal Saltonstall's office, Chilson Leonard's craggy face, McCall Maxwell's room. I saw myself curled up on my bed alone in my room at Exeter, wide awake, staring out the window, not knowing what was happening to me or how it would end. I could hear the voices in those scenes clearly, Mr. Leonard's gruff bass, Mr. Maxwell's cultivated tenor, Dad's whine. After clearing my desk at my law firm on Friday evening of that week, I took out a clean yellow pad and began to write feverishly. I now wanted to get it out of me and down on the paper where I could see it. I wrote for hours and left my office bone weary after five a.m. on Saturday morning.

When Jewelle returned on Sunday, I gave her my handwritten draft—a thick bunch of yellow pages I'd stapled along the edge like a book. She was too tired to read it carefully then, she said squinting at my scrawl, but she'd read it the next day, which she did. As she read, I watched her hunched over the manuscript, not sure what her reaction would be. I was very anxious, not because I was afraid that my writing, or the story, wasn't interesting, but anxious because I was revealing things I hadn't digested and had buried somewhere very deep. I was afraid that she would think less of me and lose respect for me because, maybe, she'd feel that I'd done something terribly wrong. But, what did I do wrong? That wasn't clear to me, despite my feeling a huge burden of guilt. I didn't feel—as I hoped I would—relief that, wow, it's all out now and I'm rid of it. Instead, I wanted to get the manuscript back—rip it out of her hands—and destroy it. But, I didn't do that. When she'd finished, she looked at me intently. She had tears in her eyes.

'Well," I asked, "what are you thinking?"

"How did you survive?

FIFTY YEARS HAVE now passed since my last encounter with Chilson Leonard in the fall of 1957. Almost everyone in my story is dead.

CHILSON LEONARD DIED in 1982 at the age of eighty, fifteen years after he'd retired from Exeter. His "Memorial Minute," an internal Exeter obituary, noted that "… [as] a person of pronounced temperament, Chilson never found living easy." I could certainly agree with "…pronounced temperament"—whatever that meant. The Memorial Minute concluded that:

> "…despite the limitations of increasing age and the
> crippling effects of arthritis, his retirement years…gave
> his useful and influential and sometimes troubled life a
> serene close."

"Sometimes troubled life"? What did the writer mean? Did he know my story or others like it? I doubt I'll ever know and, aside from that one opaque reference, I have no reason to believe anything other than that he retired as a highly-valued, maybe even celebrated, member of the Exeter faculty. Perhaps his portrait now hangs on a wall somewhere at Exeter, but I won't look for it. Maybe, my experience at his hands was unique. Maybe, he was able to control his demons in all but his dealings with me. That seems unlikely but I don't know of anyone else who ran afoul of his rage.

WILLIAM SALTONSTALL RETIRED as Principal of Exeter in 1963 when he became director of the Peace Corps in Nigeria. After two years, he returned to his home in Marion, Massachusetts, eventually teaching in the elementary school there, which I found to be amazing, but wonderful. He died in 1989 at the age of eighty-four.

I'VE BEEN TOLD that Phillips Stevens was asked to retire as Headmaster of Williston by the board of trustees in 1971, when Williston Academy merged with The Northampton School for Girls to form The Williston Northampton School, but he refused. I can understand how hard it would be for him to leave the place he felt that he had single-handedly created over more than twenty-three years. How could he leave? I'm sure he thought it was an absurd notion. His refusal provoked a crisis, especially when a new headmaster was appointed by the trustees but the new man had to deal with the fact that Mr. Stevens and his wife still resided in The Homestead, the headmaster's house—once the home of the founder, Samuel Williston. Reason finally prevailed, however, and Mr. Stevens accepted retirement in 1972, moved out of The Homestead and went to live in Old Saybrook, Connecticut. In retirement, he founded what is now the *Head's Letter*, a monthly newsletter about private schools for headmasters and headmistresses around the world. I can't imagine that his was an altogether happy retirement, although I truly hope it was. He died in Florida in 1992 at age eighty.

I NEVER LEARNED anything more than is in the book about McCall Maxwell or why he chose suicide. I knew that he'd returned from the Army after World War II—had he really been an interpreter for Generals Eisenhower and De Gaulle—was that true?—and began teaching at Lake Forest Country Day School, eventually becoming its Head. I don't know why he left that job and joined Williston as its Assistant Headmaster the year before I arrived. At my fiftieth reunion in June 2007, I told a few of my returning classmates about my experience with Mr. Maxwell. One immediately exclaimed: "Everyone knew he was a fag!" Not so, said several others, and what's more, we didn't know what a "fag" was then, which was certainly true in my case. Another classmate wondered whether there was an underground group of male and female homosexual teachers at Smith, Mount Holyoke, UMass and Amherst; maybe, Mr. Maxwell was part of a group like that? No one had any evidence of such a group or had even heard any rumors of its existence. All I am sure of is that Mr. Maxwell was gay and that his homosexuality was at the root of his fatal breakdown. He was a tragic victim of the intolerance of the time, an intolerance which persists even today, although less universally as time goes on, but, regrettably, it's still there. I will remember McCall Maxwell as a person who was tremendously important to me, who helped me at the lowest point in my young life and who genuinely seemed to care about what happened to me in this world. I choose to remember him fondly, and always will.

SOME OF THE friends I've written about are still alive and so I've given them pseudonyms lest they be unhappily surprised by their appearance here. Two of my best friends, both of whom figure importantly in my memoir, have died and don't need anonymity any longer. "Peter Bradford" is Peter Benchley, the famous author of *Jaws*. I remember that he told me once that the name given to him at birth was Bradford Peter Benchley and that he'd change it legally someday to Peter Bradford Benchley. I don't know if he did that, but I changed it for him, and just dropped the Benchley part of it for this book which was written almost completely while he was alive and, therefore, needed a pseudonym. For several years, Peter suffered from a rare and terrible progressive lung disease. I called him in January 2006 and was shocked to hear how much his usual strong, affable and slightly ironic voice had been reduced to a painfully-forced, feeble whisper. I asked him if there was anything I could do for him, truly hoping there was something. "Sure, how about a new pair of lungs?" he gasped. He was on a transplant list but the lungs never arrived. Peter died in February 2006.

LARRY FRASER, MY roommate at Exeter, went on to Cornell. I heard he'd gotten a full scholarship to play football. I hadn't seen him since I'd left Exeter but I'd always hoped to catch up with him and renew our solid friendship, perhaps when Cornell came to Cambridge to play Harvard. But, sadly, that never happened. I believe he was killed in an automobile accident in 1969.

I'VE WONDERED FROM time to time how I would have fared without the friendship and counsel of Dr. Kertess. I know his interest in me was extremely important to me, and I knew it then. I continued to see him, sometimes joined by Mrs. Kertess—Kate—

during vacations from school and college. I particularly enjoyed having lunch with him at the Café Chauveron, then one of New York's best restaurants, where he had a table reserved for him every weekday and was a favorite customer of the owner, Roger Chauveron. After Jewelle and I were married in 1962 (she, also, had been taken in under his wing—a strange coincidence), we didn't see him as often partly because we now lived in New York City and partly because the Kertesses had a young daughter, Barbara, born in 1955, and Dr. Kertess doted on her. In 1960, I met Dr. Kertess at the Park Hotel in Frankfurt where he was staying on a business trip and had brought Mrs. Kertess and Barbara with him. He had a meeting one evening and couldn't join us for dinner, which left me to entertain five-year-old Barbara at dinner. When we were given menus in German, Barbara asked me if I could read German. "No," I said. "Hm," she mused. "I'm too young to read yet but I do speak German, so I'll have the waiter read me the menu in German and I'll translate for you. You tell me what you want in English and I'll tell the waiter in German." While she was announcing her plan, she looked at me with great pity or disdain, I don't know which, but I do remember how dumb I felt.

In 1965, Dr. Kertess had a stroke and, after lingering paralyzed and unable to move or communicate—a cruelly ironic fate for this man who delighted in communicating—Mrs. Kertess took him to Germany in the hope that he could benefit from a certain therapy, but he died there in 1966 at the age of sixty-seven.

APART FROM DR. KERTESS (and Gil Hodges), there is only one unalloyed hero in my story: Fred L. Glimp. Mr. Glimp went on to have a wonderful career at Harvard becoming, in due course, Dean of Admissions and Financial Aid, the Dean of Harvard College and Vice President for Alumni Affairs and Development. *Harvard Magazine* announced in its September-October 2004 issue that he and his wife (known as "Buster") had been "...honored by the creation of a Faculty of Arts and Sciences professorship in economics, government, or history" and called him "prodigiously successful." He is alive and well, living in Cambridge, Massachusetts and, supposedly, retired. He told me, when I called him to tell him about this book, that his wife accuses him of having failed retirement—he keeps getting, and accepting, assignments to do things for Harvard. I'm sure that he is continuing to do good things for Harvard. He seemed pleased when I told him what a good thing he'd done for me.

MOM DIED IN Columbia Presbyterian Medical Center in New York City on New Years Eve at the end of 1978. She was seventy-two. She had cancer, but it was a heart attack she'd had during the night that killed her—and, I'm sure, the years and years of alcoholism. I went to the hospital that day and talked to her doctors. They opened the door of her private room and I saw her on the hospital bed wrapped like a mummy in white cloth with her arms at her sides. The white wrapping went under her chin and around the top of her head covering her hair completely but leaving her face exposed. I thought she looked like a nun, and a young one at that. Her face had lost its alcoholic puffiness and, with it, decades of age. She looked very much as she had when the photograph I mentioned in the book had been taken. She looked beautiful and serene. It is a good image of her for me to remember. It helps me deal with the anger I still feel when I think of how alcohol robbed her of so much that she could have done. But, is that true? Could she have accomplished very much? The times were certainly against her. She had no money at all of her own and was totally financially dependent on my secretive father who gave her an allowance and never told her if they were rich or poor. She had no education, for in the days when she was growing up it was very unusual to educate a daughter, although her oldest sister, my Aunt Mary whose husband Lloyd got blamed for killing Mom's Rambler, did go to college. In fact, I think Mom did a great deal with what she had to deal with and I no longer blame her for anesthetizing herself every day. I still feel love for her and an overwhelming sadness that her life had not been happier.

AFTER FORTY-EIGHT YEARS at the same Wall Street law firm, Simpson, Thacher & Bartlett, Dad retired in 1975, when he was seventy-four and, he thought, sure to die pretty soon after that. He'd had to retire because his vision had deteriorated due to a condition caused, his doctor told him, by smoking cigarettes. Nicotine had constricted the blood vessels feeding his optic nerve and that produced holes in his vision; he could not see anything that he was looking at directly. When he tried to read something, he had to look all around the page using his peripheral vision. In some ways, he became a better and faster reader, but it was very tiring. During his last years to the law firm, he'd have younger lawyers read cases and the drafts of their briefs to him.

Since he had no hobbies or avocations whatsoever and the only sport he enjoyed was curling once a week during the winter, he didn't know what he would do in retirement, and neither did we. What happened was that during the first days, weeks and months of his retirement, he'd sit in the same chair in the den of our house and watch Mom going about her daily routine as if he weren't there. He quickly became very critical of her ways, belittling the importance of whatever she did and berating her for spending so much time having lunch with her friends. His attacks drove her deeper and deeper into her alcoholism until, less than a year before she died, she finally decided that she couldn't deal with alcohol anymore and checked herself into a rehabilitation clinic in White Plains. She stopped drinking entirely for a few days—maybe, even a few weeks—and then started having wine with her dinner, then with her lunch and dinner and was soon drinking a prodigious amount of chardonnay.

After she died, Dad became Mom in a stunningly ironic adaptation. Her friends became his friends, which was good because he didn't have any friends of his own. And, the lunches with Mom's pals continued, frequently at our house, the only difference being that Dad took Mom's place. His entire life became centered on those women and they seemed to enjoy him as much as he needed them, although he would never admit that. Every year, Dad would go into something very like mourning on New Year's Eve remembering Mom. He wouldn't go out on New Year's Day and make the traditional round of eggnog parties. His evident sadness seemed peculiar to me. It seemed clear that he had strong feelings for her, feelings that I never saw him express in any way during her life.

Eventually, he outlived all but the youngest of Mom's friends and they immeasurably brightened his retirement which covered the last twenty-two years of his life. He lived to see four of his grandchildren—my two girls and Bob's older son and daughter —grow into adulthood and to know Bob's younger twin sons and to hold his first great granddaughter, my daughter Emily Lansbury's daughter, Elizabeth Laura, but not her sister Natalie Rose, who was born eight months after Dad died. He became the oldest human being I've ever known. His hands became like gnarled driftwood sticking out from the sleeves of his usual plaid flannel shirt. His legs became wobbly and for the last few years of his life he wasn't able to take his usual walk around the fields of Nevis Labs across the street from our house in Ardsley-on-Hudson.

One morning when he was ninety-six, he got out of bed before the sun was up, got dressed and went to the top of the stairs to use the stair chair lift he'd installed to go downstairs as usual. But, when he went to sit in the chair, he missed and went tumbling head over heals down the stairs. His doctor couldn't find anything broken or even bruised when he rushed to our house and examined Dad but he didn't trust himself. He put Dad in the hospital anyway, sure that X-rays or other diagnostic equipment available there would show that he'd damaged something—ninety-six-year-old people just can't somersault down steep stairs and not hurt themselves. However, nothing was found during the week he was in the hospital but he never walked again after that stay; the muscles in his scrawny legs atrophied and whatever physical therapy he could do wasn't sufficient to rebuild them. From that time on, he began to lapse into waking trances in which he'd be in some other place and time. I was sure he was recalling memories from long ago with an astounding degree of detail. Once, when I entered his room to see him, I found him in bed lying flat, staring at the ceiling and singing a song in a thin, wavering but bright voice. He didn't acknowledge me and I was sure he wasn't aware of me. He was somewhere else, singing with someone he liked. He was having fun. I listened to all the bawdy words. He sang with fragile gusto and never hesitated with any of the lyrics that I am positive he had not sung since the 1920's. When he was done, he closed his eyes and went to sleep with a smile on his face. That's how I want to remember him, not with the pained, sardonic grimace I think he may have had on his face during my entire adolescence. He died in November 1998, a month short of his ninety-seventh birthday.

I THINK BOB became my best male friend during my sophomore year at Harvard when he was at the law school there. I remember asking him to have dinner with me at the Wursthaus, an ersatz German restaurant just off Harvard Square. I was taking a music composition course and that, together with a wonderful discovery I'd made, had inflamed me with a passion to be a composer. My discovery was of a huge Steinway concert grand piano improbably located in the small room in the cupola at the very top of Eliot House, where I lived with five roommates, including Peter Benchley, in two adjoining suites. I don't remember now why I wandered up the long flights of narrow stairs behind the dining hall to that room, but I came to believe that it was a beneficent Providence that led me there. There was nothing in the room, which I remember as being about twenty feet square with a huge round window that looked out over the Charles River, except that magnificent piano and a bench. I went up there in the day and at night at any hour and never found another soul there in the three years I enjoyed that room. It was my secret room and I didn't tell anyone about it, lest it prove to be a beautiful mirage and vanish. That night at the Wursthaus, I asked Bob, after a number of beers, what he thought Dad would do if I told him that I wanted to be a composer. Bob wasn't in doubt. He thought the Old Man would have a fit; I believe he mentioned cutting off my tuition and allowance; maybe disinheritance was mentioned. Whatever he told me, I left dinner that night with no illusion that Dad would support me in pursuing my passion. I listened to Bob, who suggested I make music an important hobby, remain an English major and later go to law school—that's what Dad would support, he thought. I followed his advice but also kept at my music over the years, writing simple things that were performed at Jewelle's and my twenty-fifth wedding anniversary in 1987, and at the weddings of each of my daughters. Now, after having retired from practicing law, I am composing again whenever I can.

I've always respected Bob's amazing intelligence when he was doing problem-solving things like crossword puzzles. He had a huge amount of information at his fingertips and a great sense of humor. But, I wondered about his judgment, based on the time he tried to kill me and later, die with me. But, that night at the Wursthaus, I came to admire his calm good judgment. He became more than my big brother then, a good and honest advisor and friend. And those feelings have lasted throughout all the years when we both were practicing law at different firms and then, for about five years, together. Many times I have wished that Bob was happier than I suspected him to be and that he'd made a few different choices in his life. I don't think his career as a lawyer was as fulfilling for him as he'd hoped it would be. But, I do think he's found something in retirement that eluded him before: a sense of worth and purpose in serving, sometimes as pro bono legal counsel, a number of organizations in and around Cold Spring, NY—the Hudson Riverkeeper and the local historical society to mention two—and continue his long involvement with the Blue Hill Troupe and the Canterbury Choral Society in New York City.

As FOR ME, I didn't just survive; I thrived, through college at Harvard and law school at Columbia. Midway through my first year at Columbia, I married Jewelle, then a junior at Randolph-Macon Woman's College in Virginia, who is the best person I have ever known. Marrying her was, and still is, the best thing I've ever done, although I have definitely challenged her and been challenged by her throughout our, now, almost forty-six-year marriage.

When I first met Jewelle in the fall of 1957, what struck me most about her was her unquenchable life force. It struck me as physically as if it had been a huge wave or a hurricane gust, and it bowled me over. While we weren't married until February 1962, I had known from the time I met her that I couldn't live without her, or at least did not want to try. The night of my twenty-first birthday party in January 1961, I told Betty, my parents' Irish leprechaun housekeeper who'd raised me, that I was going to marry Jewelle. "Is that so?" she said. "Well, then. I'd better take a good look at her, hadn't I now?" And she did take a look, and she approved highly. "When will the wedding be," she asked?

"When I ask her, I hope," I replied. I did ask her that fall and, thank God, she said yes. The refrain of a song I wrote for her for our 25th anniversary goes: "I love you more every day." And, I believe that is still true today. She is my best friend and wisest advisor. She is also fun to be with, always stimulating and always looking for, and finding, important new things to do and people to meet. Her energy is prodigious and her insight and intuition laser-like. My life would have been dull without her and has been gloriously rich and interesting because of her.

AFTER GRADUATION FROM law school, I joined Cahill, Gordon & Reindel, the one big Wall Street law firm that Dad hated. He'd come up against Cahill, Gordon on the other side of an antitrust case and thought them uncouth. The main Cahill, Gordon partner, a rough and brilliant litigator named John Sonnett, apparently made a monkey out of the Simpson, Thacher partner in charge of the case, and Dad never forgot, or forgave, it. He gasped when I told him I'd accepted a job there.

I had an astonishingly interesting six years at Cahill, Gordon, several of which were spent in the firm's small Washington, D.C. outpost, working for John Sonnett, Dad's *bête noire*, who became Senior Partner of the firm on the death of John Cahill in 1966. Most unfortunately, John Sonnett died of brain cancer in 1968. When he died I lost my guru, friend and mentor. I was devastated by his death. I was also out-of-sync at the firm in New York, having spent so much time working for John and living in Washington, and felt that I no longer belonged there. I left in 1970 and joined John Lankenau and Victor Kovner, friends from Ed Koch's first congressional campaign, to form Lankenau,

Kovner & Bickford. We practiced happily and precariously together for twenty-two years. I felt incredibly lucky in the variety
of the problems and clients that came my way during those years:
artists, art dealers and galleries; venture capitalists and struggling entrepreneurs; writers and book and magazine publishers;
gold prospectors; commodity speculators; speed-reading schools
and day-care centers; sewer cleaners; dog groomers; inventors;
many hedge funds and a mutual fund; investment advisors, bro-
ker-dealers, investment bankers and even the government of a
foreign country.

By 1992, the world had changed and become more complicated.
I moved back to a larger mainstream firm, Lane & Mittendorf,
which had tax lawyers and other specialists. It merged with another mid-sized firm to form Windels, Marx, Lane & Mittendorf
on January 1, 2000. I became "of counsel" to the firm in 2002
and retired completely in 2005.

I LOVE EVERY day of my life, or at least most of them. When I'm
not writing, I go back to composing music on the piano, which
I still play poorly, or an electronic synthesizer, which contains
a vast world of sounds and can keep me occupied for hours. I
travel a fair amount with Jewelle (but not on her three-day business round trips to London or Paris as a wonderfully creative
Global Partner with the Rothschild family's investment bank-
ing firm), am on a few boards and committees and do the best I
can to read a great deal—I've read scores of memoirs in the past
few years—and to stay current with the important events in this
ever-changing and always-challenging world. I also try to stay
in touch with my brilliant, beautiful and busy daughters: Laura,

the producer of *Traffic*, which won four Oscars, two films about Che Guevara to be released in 2008 and many other major pictures, who lives in Hollywood with her husband, Sam Bottoms, an actor who debuted in *The Last Picture Show* and was Lance the Surfer in *Apocalypse Now*, among a great many other roles; and, our younger daughter, Emily, a budding movie producer looking for books from which to make good movies for children and young adults, who lives in Garrison, New York, with her wonderful husband, George Lansbury, the product of a theatrical family that includes his famous aunt, Angela, producer father, Edgar, and actor brother, David. George is an executive at Cablevision in charge of all programming for one of its HDTV channels. Emily and George are the parents of our two perfect granddaughters, Elizabeth Laura, now thirteen, and Natalie Rose, now eight. I am most happily surrounded by women, having two daughters and now two granddaughters; even my dog, Penny, is female! We spend as much of the summers as possible together at our house on Mishaum Point on Buzzards Bay in South Dartmouth, Massachusetts—wonderful summers that get shorter and shorter as the years go by.

New York, New York
March 2008